How to be a man

Foreword

Hello there!

You've just picked up a book that's more than words on pages. It's a journey, a challenge, and a promise. This isn't your everyday advice book. It's a guide to unlocking the strong, confident man within you.

Why did I write this book? Because I've been where you are. Searching for answers, looking for ways to be better, stronger, and more fulfilled. I discovered that the path to true manhood is through growth, understanding, and action. And now, I want to share that path with you. 💪

In these pages, you'll find the keys to:

- Boosting your health and understanding the power of your body.
- Building meaningful connections that enrich your life. 👫
- Discovering the joy of moving your body and strengthening your mind. 🧠
- Navigating the digital world with purpose and control. 📱
- Embracing challenges and staying productive. ✍️
- Finding your confidence and standing tall in who you are. 💪

This book is your toolkit for life. It's packed with science-backed advice, real-life strategies, and stories to inspire you. Whether you're looking to improve your health, your relationships, or your mindset, you'll find guidance here.

But remember, reading is just the start. The real magic happens when you take action. Each chapter is designed to push you, challenge you, and help you grow. From mastering your emotions to leading with courage, you're about to start the adventure of a lifetime.

So, are you ready to be the man you're meant to be? To face life with confidence, wisdom, and strength? Let's dive in. The journey to greatness begins now. Let's turn these pages into steps towards your legendary legacy. 🏆

Welcome to your transformation. Welcome to "How Can You Unlock Your True Potential?" Let's make it awesome. Let's make it strong.

Your journey starts now. Let's go! 🚀 📖

Table of Contents

Foreword 2
The Importance of Testosterone 7
The Importance of Diet 21
The Importance of Companionship 25
The Importance of Working out 27
The Importance of Handling social media 39
The Importance of Being busy 44
The Importance of Conquering Fears 48
The Importance of Self-Confidence 52
The Importance of Masculinity 56
The Importance of Loyalty 60
The Importance of Stoicism 63
The Importance of Purpose 66
The Importance of Self-Care 69
The Importance of Being alone 73
The Importance of Hardship 77
The Importance of Taking Risks 80
The Importance of Saying No 83
The Importance of Money 85
The Importance of Becoming Smarter 88
The Importance of Life Experience 91
The Importance of Staying Away From Porn 94
The Importance of Adaptability 97

The Importance of Patience.. 100
The Art of Decision Making.. 103
The Art of Storytelling.. 105
The Art of Being Independent... 110
The Art of Negotiation... 113
Cultivating Leadership Skills... 116
Developing Critical Thinking Skills..................................... 121
Developing Emotional Resilience....................................... 123
Developing a Positive Mindset... 126
Developing Persistence... 129
Developing a Sense of Humor.. 134
Dealing with Peer Pressure... 137
Experiences That Forge a Man.. 139
Leaving a Legacy.. 141
A Man's Happiness... 146
Do Something.. 148
Inspiring Movies.. 151
When to Start Dating?.. 154
What to look for in a woman?... 156
How to Behave Around a Woman?..................................... 158
Checklist: Am I a good man?... 161

Introduction

Welcome to "How to Be a Man" – a guide that ventures beyond the conventional, delves into the controversial, and strikes at the heart of what it means to be a modern man. This book isn't your typical self-help guide filled with generic advice. It's a raw, unfiltered journey into the depths of manhood, crafted to resonate with you on a deeply emotional level.

Who is this book for? It's for the man who feels lost in the noise of conflicting advice on what masculinity should look like. It's for the guy who wants more than just surface-level tips on attracting a partner or maintaining fitness. It's for the individual who's ready to confront uncomfortable truths, challenge societal norms, and redefine what it means to be a man in today's world.

Throughout these pages, we'll tackle topics that many shy away from. We'll discuss the role of testosterone, dissect the concept of a 'good woman', and provide unorthodox advice on attracting a partner. We'll confront the idea of being a 'simp' head-on and explore the crucial role of fitness in a man's life. And beyond these, we will delve into the nuances of maintaining relationships, emotional resilience, and personal growth.

This book is not about telling you what you want to hear. It's about telling you what you need to hear. Expect to be challenged. Expect to question. And expect to embark on a journey that will take you through every facet of your life as a man.

So, buckle up. It's time to dive in and explore the unvarnished truth about being a man.

The Importance of Testosterone

Testosterone - the very word conjures images of strength, vitality, and masculinity. But what exactly is this heralded substance that seems to be the bedrock of manhood? Testosterone is a steroid hormone predominantly produced in the testicles of males. It's not just a chemical in your body; it's the architect of your masculinity, shaping both your physical and psychological landscape.

The Multifaceted Power of Testosterone

Muscle Mass and Strength:
Testosterone is like a natural bodybuilder within you. It plays a critical role in building and maintaining muscle mass and strength. This isn't just about looking good - it's about feeling powerful, capable, and ready to face life's challenges.

Bone Density:
Your bones are the framework of your body, and testosterone acts as their strengthener. Higher testosterone levels contribute to denser, stronger bones, reducing the risk of osteoporosis and fractures as you age.

Thicker Skin:
Literally, testosterone contributes to thicker skin compared to women, providing better protection and faster healing. It's nature's armor, guarding you against the physical scrapes of life.

Confidence and Mental Fortitude:
Testosterone wields influence over your mind too. It's linked to higher levels of confidence, assertiveness, and a lower likelihood of depression. It's like a natural antidepressant, bolstering your mental resilience.

Hair Growth:
Testosterone is responsible for male-pattern hair growth, including facial, chest, and limb hair. It's the signature of your manliness, setting you apart in the realm of physical attributes.

Fat Distribution and Metabolism:
Testosterone helps regulate body fat distribution and metabolism, making it easier to build muscle and burn fat. It's your natural ally in staying fit and maintaining a healthy physique.

Libido and Sexual Health:
At its core, testosterone drives your sexual desire and function. It's crucial for maintaining a healthy libido and plays a significant role in erectile health.

Cardiovascular Health:
Testosterone has a significant role in maintaining a healthy heart and blood vessels, thus contributing to overall cardiovascular health.

Mood Regulation:
It's not all about the physical; testosterone significantly impacts your mood and overall sense of well-being.

Cognitive Function:
Testosterone influences certain cognitive abilities, including memory and concentration.

Energy Levels:
This hormone is integral in maintaining high energy levels and stamina, crucial for everyday activities and overall vitality.

Enhanced Scent Perception and Personal Odor:
Testosterone can subtly influence body odor, potentially making it more appealing to others. This is due to its effect on pheromone production, which plays a role in social and sexual communication.

While "smelling better" is subjective, hormonal balance can influence personal scent in a way that may be perceived as more attractive.

Quicker Fat Loss:
Testosterone plays a crucial role in regulating fat distribution and metabolism. Higher levels of testosterone can enhance the body's ability to burn fat, making weight loss efforts more effective. This is particularly evident in the reduction of visceral fat, which is closely linked to metabolic health risks.

Emotional Control:
Higher testosterone levels have been associated with increased emotional resilience and control. This hormone can influence how the brain regulates emotions, leading to a more balanced emotional state and better stress management.

Enhanced Tolerance to Temperature Extremes:
Testosterone may contribute to the body's ability to regulate its temperature, offering better endurance in facing both cold and warmth. This enhanced tolerance can be particularly beneficial in environments that require physical resilience.

Deeper Voice:
Testosterone affects the vocal cords, leading to a deeper voice, a trait often associated with masculinity. During puberty, increased testosterone levels result in the thickening of the vocal cords, which lowers the pitch of the voice.

Improved Cognitive Function:
Beyond its physical benefits, testosterone has been linked to cognitive abilities. Higher levels of testosterone are associated with improvements in memory, spatial abilities, and mathematical reasoning.

Increased Energy and Vitality:
Testosterone is vital for overall energy levels and vitality. It influences the body's energy metabolism, contributing to a feeling of vigor and reducing the sensation of fatigue.

Muscle Endurance and Recovery:
Testosterone enhances muscle endurance and recovery after exercise, allowing for more intense and prolonged physical activities. This is due to its role in muscle protein synthesis and overall muscular health.

Skin Health and Healing:
Beyond contributing to thicker skin, testosterone plays a role in skin health and the healing process. It can improve the skin's appearance and accelerate the healing of wounds.

Enhanced Immune System Function:
Some research suggests that testosterone has a role in immune system regulation. It can influence the body's defense mechanisms, although the exact effects can vary and depend on a balance with other hormones.

Imagine a world where you're at the peak of your testosterone levels. You feel unstoppable, ready to conquer every challenge. Your body is robust, your mind sharp, and your confidence sky-high. That's the power of testosterone.

But it's not just about reaching the peak; it's about maintaining it. As men age, testosterone levels naturally decline, leading to a host of issues like fatigue, weight gain, and decreased libido. It's like watching the sun set on your prime years – but it doesn't have to be that way.

You hold the power to boost and maintain your testosterone levels. How? Through lifestyle choices – regular exercise, particularly strength training and high-intensity workouts, and a diet rich in proteins and healthy fats. Think of foods like lean meats, eggs, and nuts as fuel for your testosterone engine.

Understanding the Impact of Low Testosterone

While we've explored the myriad benefits of testosterone, it's equally crucial to understand the consequences of low testosterone levels, not just on your physical health but on your behavior and mental state as well.

Low testosterone, or 'Low T,' can manifest in various subtle yet impactful ways:

Physical Fatigue and Weakness:
One of the most noticeable signs of low testosterone is a general feeling of fatigue and a decrease in muscle strength. This isn't just about feeling tired; it's about losing the zest and energy that propels you through life's daily activities.

Weight Gain and Muscle Loss:
Low testosterone makes it harder to maintain muscle mass and easier to gain fat, particularly around the abdomen. This shift in body composition can lead to a negative self-image and a decrease in physical fitness.

Reduced Libido and Sexual Dysfunction:
A decline in sexual desire and difficulties with sexual performance can be a direct consequence of low testosterone, affecting not just physical intimacy but also emotional connections and self-esteem.

Mood Swings and Depression:
Testosterone influences mood regulation. Low levels can lead to feelings of sadness, irritability, and a lack of motivation, impacting not

just your mental health but also your relationships and everyday interactions.

Cognitive Difficulties:
Concentration and memory can also take a hit. You might find it harder to focus, remember things, or make decisions, which can affect your work and personal life.

Decreased Bone Density:
Over time, low testosterone can lead to weaker bones, increasing the risk of fractures and osteoporosis.

Increased Body Fat and Metabolic Syndrome:
Low T levels are often associated with an increase in body fat. This hormonal imbalance can also predispose individuals to metabolic syndrome, a cluster of conditions that increase the risk of heart disease, stroke, and type 2 diabetes.

Thinning Hair or Hair Loss:
Testosterone plays a role in hair production. Low levels can lead to thinning hair on the scalp, face, and body.

Decreased Energy Levels:
Beyond general fatigue, low testosterone can lead to a profound lack of energy, making it difficult to engage in regular activities and exercise, further exacerbating health issues.

Sleep Disturbances:
Low T can contribute to sleep disorders, including insomnia and disrupted sleep patterns, which can significantly impact overall health and mood.

Emotional Instability:
Beyond mood swings and depression, low testosterone can lead to emotional instability, decreased motivation, and feelings of hopelessness.

Decreased Sense of Well-Being:
Individuals with low T often report a general decline in their sense of well-being, including lower confidence and a pessimistic outlook on life.

Reduced Semen Volume:
Testosterone plays a critical role in semen production. Lower levels can lead to a decrease in semen volume, affecting fertility.

Changes in Cholesterol and Lipid Levels:
Testosterone influences lipid metabolism. Low levels can lead to unfavorable changes in cholesterol levels, increasing cardiovascular risk.

Increased Inflammation:
Some studies suggest that low testosterone levels are associated with increased markers of inflammation, which is linked to various chronic conditions.

Impact on Skin Health:
Testosterone influences skin health; lower levels can lead to dryer, less elastic skin, contributing to the appearance of aging.

Anemia:
Testosterone stimulates red blood cell production. A deficiency can lead to anemia, characterized by fatigue and weakness.

Gynecomastia:
Low testosterone levels can upset the hormonal balance, leading to increased breast tissue in men, a condition known as gynecomastia.

Reduced Exercise Tolerance:
Low T can decrease one's ability to tolerate exercise, reducing physical performance and making it challenging to engage in regular physical activity.

Impact on Mental Acuity:
Testosterone influences cognitive functions. Low levels have been linked to a decline in mental acuity, including slower processing speeds and difficulty in learning new information.

But beyond these physical and psychological effects, low testosterone can subtly influence your behavior and how you interact with the world, particularly in the realm of relationships and social dynamics. One term that's gained traction in popular culture is "simping" – a behavior characterized by excessive subservience or attention to others, often in the hope of winning their affection or favor, particularly in the context of romantic or sexual pursuits.

While "simping" is a complex and multifaceted behavior influenced by many factors beyond just hormonal levels, testosterone does play a role in assertiveness, confidence, and social dominance. Low testosterone might contribute to a lack of confidence, making you more likely to seek approval or validation from others in ways that might not align with your true self.

This is not about casting judgment or labeling behaviors but about understanding the profound impact hormones can have on our actions and perceptions. Recognizing these effects is the first step in addressing them. For those experiencing symptoms of low testosterone, it's crucial to consult with a healthcare professional. They can provide guidance on medical interventions, lifestyle changes, and dietary adjustments that can help in restoring testosterone levels and, consequently, your vigor, confidence, and well-being.

The Life-Changing Power of High Testosterone

Imagine waking up each day with a reservoir of energy, a mind as sharp as a tack, and a body that's primed and ready for action. That's the power of high testosterone. This isn't just about having more of a hormone; it's about unlocking a version of yourself that's primed to excel, to conquer, to thrive. Testosterone, in its optimal levels, isn't just a component of your biology – it's a catalyst for a life lived fuller, stronger, and with more vitality.

Why High Testosterone is Your Ally for a Better Life

Unmatched Energy and Vitality:
High testosterone fuels your body with the energy it needs to tackle everything from rigorous workouts to long days at work. It's like having a natural source of high-octane fuel that keeps you running at peak performance.

Sharper Mental Clarity and Focus:
This hormone isn't just about brawn; it also contributes to your brainpower. With high testosterone levels, you might find yourself more focused, with a sharper memory and quicker cognitive functions. It's like upgrading your brain to a faster, more efficient processor.

Elevated Mood and Confidence:
High testosterone can be a game-changer for your mental and emotional well-being. It's often associated with higher levels of confidence, optimism, and overall satisfaction with life. Imagine walking into any room, any situation, and feeling like you own it – that's the confidence we're talking about.

Enhanced Physical Strength and Muscle Mass:
This is where testosterone really shines. It aids in building and maintaining muscle mass, making your workouts more effective and

your physique more robust. It's not just about looking great (though that's a definite perk); it's about feeling powerful and capable.

Improved Sexual Health and Libido:
Testosterone is essential for a healthy sex drive and sexual function. High levels mean a more robust libido and better sexual health, aspects that play a critical role in your relationships and overall quality of life.

Better Body Composition:
High testosterone makes it easier to manage your weight, helping in maintaining a healthier ratio of muscle to fat. This isn't just about vanity; it's about the profound impact a healthy body composition has on your health, from reducing the risk of chronic diseases to improving your physical agility and endurance.

Stronger Bones:
This hormone plays a crucial role in bone density. Stronger bones mean a sturdier, more resilient body, reducing the risk of fractures and osteoporosis, especially as you age.

Social Dominance and Leadership Qualities:
Testosterone is often linked to traits like leadership, assertiveness, and social dominance. It's about having the natural charisma and confidence to lead, influence, and inspire those around you.

Emotional Resilience:
With high testosterone, you're not just physically robust; you're also mentally tougher. It can help in fostering resilience against stress, anxiety, and depression, equipping you to handle life's ups and downs with greater composure.

Improved Recovery Times:
Elevated testosterone levels can significantly reduce recovery time after workouts, allowing you to train harder and more frequently. This

rapid recovery supports consistent progress in your physical goals and reduces the risk of injury, keeping you on track toward achieving peak physical condition.

Increased Competitiveness and Motivation:
Testosterone naturally enhances your drive to succeed and compete, whether in sports, at work, or in personal endeavors. This heightened competitiveness comes with increased motivation, pushing you to set and achieve higher goals, and to persist in the face of challenges.

Enhanced Heart Health:
Testosterone has a protective effect on the heart, contributing to the health of cardiac muscle and reducing the risk of heart disease. Adequate levels of this hormone are associated with a healthier lipid profile, improved blood flow, and lower blood pressure, all of which are vital for long-term cardiovascular health.

Regulation of Blood Sugar:
High testosterone levels play a role in regulating insulin sensitivity and blood sugar levels, reducing the risk of developing type 2 diabetes. By aiding in the maintenance of a healthy weight and muscle mass, testosterone helps in preventing insulin resistance, a major factor in diabetes.

Optimal Immune System Function:
Testosterone can bolster your immune response, offering better protection against infections and diseases. While the relationship between hormones and immune function is complex, adequate testosterone levels are linked to a more robust immune system.

Increased Pain Tolerance:
Studies suggest that high testosterone levels can increase your pain tolerance, allowing you to push through discomfort during workouts or recover more comfortably from injuries. This enhanced pain tolerance supports more effective training sessions and a more active lifestyle.

Improved Skin Health:
Testosterone contributes to skin elasticity and density, reducing the appearance of aging and promoting a healthier, more vibrant complexion. Its role in skin health means fewer wrinkles, less sagging, and a more youthful appearance overall.

Sharper Visual and Spatial Abilities:
Testosterone is linked to improved visual and spatial abilities, enhancing your capacity for visualizing objects in space, which can be beneficial in both everyday tasks and specific professional or athletic endeavors.

Regulation of Mood Swings:
By maintaining high testosterone levels, you can achieve a more stable mood and reduce the likelihood of experiencing drastic mood swings. This hormonal balance is key to maintaining emotional stability and fostering a positive, proactive approach to life's challenges.

Enhanced Creativity and Risk-Taking:
Testosterone has been associated with increased creativity and a willingness to take risks. These traits can lead to innovation and success in various fields, pushing you to explore new ideas, start ventures, or tackle projects that require thinking outside the box.

Imagine the possibilities of a life where you're not just getting by, but thriving. High testosterone isn't a magic pill, but it's undeniably a powerful ally in your journey towards becoming the best version of yourself. It's about embracing a life of vitality, strength, and confidence. In the chapters ahead, we'll explore how to naturally boost and maintain your testosterone levels, so you can unlock this incredible potential within you.

Boosting Your Testosterone Naturally

Harnessing the power of testosterone is about more than understanding its benefits; it's about actively taking steps to enhance its levels in your body. Imagine turning the dial up on your masculinity, strength, and vitality. This isn't just about chasing a number in a blood test; it's about reclaiming your energy, your confidence, your very essence as a man. And the good news? You can significantly influence your testosterone levels through natural means.

Protein-Rich Foods:
Think steak, eggs, and fish. These aren't just satisfying meals; they're testosterone-boosting powerhouses. Proteins provide essential amino acids that are crucial for testosterone production.

Healthy Fats:
Your body needs fat to produce testosterone, but not just any fat. Focus on monounsaturated and omega-3 fats found in avocados, nuts, seeds, and fatty fish like salmon.

Vitamins and Minerals:
Certain vitamins and minerals play pivotal roles in testosterone production. Zinc, found in oysters and other shellfish, boosts testosterone. Vitamin D, which you can get from the sun or supplements, is also crucial.

Strength Training:
Lifting weights isn't just about building muscles; it's about signaling your body to produce more testosterone. Focus on compound movements like squats, deadlifts, and bench presses.

High-Intensity Interval Training (HIIT):
These short, intense bursts of exercise have been shown to boost testosterone levels. They're not easy, but they're incredibly effective.
Lifestyle Changes: Beyond Diet and Exercise

Stress Reduction:
Chronic stress leads to high cortisol levels, which can inhibit testosterone production. Find stress-reduction techniques that work for you, be it meditation, yoga, or simply taking time to relax.

Sleep Quality:
Testosterone is produced during sleep, making quality sleep crucial. Aim for 7-9 hours of uninterrupted sleep per night.

Limit Alcohol and Avoid Smoking:
Excessive alcohol and tobacco use can lower testosterone levels. Moderation is key.

Reduce Exposure to Endocrine Disruptors:
Certain plastics, pesticides, and other chemicals can disrupt hormonal balance. Be mindful of what you consume and how it's stored.

Supplements
While your focus should be on diet and lifestyle, certain supplements can support testosterone production. These include vitamin D, zinc, and magnesium. Always consult with a healthcare provider before starting any supplement regime.

Imagine implementing these changes and feeling the difference in your body and mind. It's about waking up each day with more energy, seeing the results in the gym, and feeling a renewed sense of confidence in every aspect of your life. This isn't just a physical transformation; it's a mental and emotional rejuvenation.

But remember, boosting testosterone naturally isn't a quick fix; it's a commitment to a healthier, stronger you. It's a journey of small, consistent changes that add up to a monumental shift in how you feel, look, and live. As you turn the pages of this book, think of each chapter as a step towards unleashing the full potential of your manhood.

The Importance of Diet

Start your journey to elevate your testosterone levels, you'll quickly find that the path is paved with what you put on your plate. Diet is not just about fueling your body; it's about crafting the very hormones that define your manhood. In this chapter, we dive deep into the role of diet, particularly the emphasis on protein and the strategic management of carbohydrates, in boosting testosterone.

The Meat of the Matter: Protein as a Testosterone Booster

Imagine your body as a high-performance vehicle. Just as this vehicle requires the right fuel to function optimally, your body needs the right nutrients to produce testosterone. At the forefront of these nutrients is protein, particularly from meat.

Why Meat?
Meat is packed with essential amino acids, the building blocks of protein, which are crucial for testosterone production. It's not just about building muscles; it's about fostering the hormonal environment that defines your masculinity.
Red meat, for instance, is rich in zinc, a mineral directly linked to increased testosterone levels. It's like hitting two birds with one stone – building muscle and boosting your hormonal health.

Variety is Key
While red meat is often highlighted, don't overlook other sources like poultry, fish, and eggs. Each type of meat brings its unique profile of nutrients, contributing to a well-rounded diet that supports testosterone production.

The Quality of Your Meat Matters
Opt for grass-fed, organic options whenever possible. These choices are not only healthier but also free from hormones and antibiotics that can disrupt your own hormonal balance.

As we delve further into the dietary foundations for boosting testosterone, it becomes crucial to understand the role of fats, minerals, and the strategic management of certain food groups. Incorporating real butter, Himalayan salt, and moderating intake of carbohydrates and vegetable oils are key strategies in this nutritional journey.

The Benefits of Real Butter
Real butter, particularly from grass-fed sources, is rich in healthy fats, including butyrate and conjugated linoleic acid (CLA), which have been shown to support testosterone production. Unlike its processed counterparts, real butter provides a host of fat-soluble vitamins (A, D, E, and K2) essential for hormonal balance and overall health. The saturated fats in butter play a crucial role in the synthesis of testosterone, debunking the myth that all saturated fats are harmful.

Himalayan Salt:
Himalayan salt, with its plethora of trace minerals (over 84 minerals and trace elements), offers more than just seasoning benefits. It aids in proper adrenal function, hydration, and electrolyte balance in the body, which are vital for maintaining optimal testosterone levels. Unlike regular table salt, which is heavily processed and stripped of most beneficial minerals, Himalayan salt supports your body's natural hormone production by providing essential minerals that act as cofactors in various biochemical processes, including testosterone synthesis.

Why to Moderate Carbohydrates
While carbohydrates are necessary for energy, their excessive consumption, especially refined carbs, can lead to insulin resistance and obesity, both of which are linked to lower testosterone levels. A balanced approach to carbohydrates, favoring complex carbs like vegetables, whole grains, and legumes, can support hormonal health without spiking insulin levels. This moderation helps in maintaining a healthy weight and optimizing testosterone production.

The Case Against Vegetable Oils
In the landscape of dietary fats, vegetable oils are frequently criticized for their high content of omega-6 fatty acids and potential trans fats, which can promote inflammation and oxidative stress, negatively impacting testosterone levels and overall health. The modern diet's skewed ratio of omega-6 to omega-3 fatty acids is a concern for hormonal balance and inflammation.

A healthier alternative to vegetable oils is real butter, especially when sourced from grass-fed cows. Unlike vegetable oils, real butter is rich in saturated fats, which are crucial for testosterone production. It also contains beneficial nutrients like butyrate, a short-chain fatty acid that can improve gut health and reduce inflammation, and conjugated linoleic acid (CLA), which has been linked to fat loss and improved metabolic health. Moreover, butter is a source of fat-soluble vitamins (A, D, E, and K2) that play essential roles in hormone synthesis and regulation.

Crafting Your Hormonal Health Through Diet
Incorporating real butter for its beneficial fats, Himalayan salt for its mineral content, moderating carbohydrate intake to avoid insulin spikes, and avoiding vegetable oils in favor of healthier fats, are all strategic dietary choices that support testosterone production. These adjustments are not just about improving hormonal health; they're about embracing a lifestyle that prioritizes natural, unprocessed foods for overall well-being.

A Closer Look at Protein Shakes
In the pursuit of muscle mass and strength, protein shakes have become a staple in many fitness enthusiasts' diets. While they offer a convenient way to increase protein intake, it's essential to scrutinize what else comes along with the protein in these supplements. This section delves into the lesser-discussed aspects of protein shakes and advocates for the benefits of natural protein sources.

The Hidden Downsides of Protein Shakes
Many protein shakes and powders, while packed with protein, also contain additives, artificial sweeteners, and preservatives that might not align with your health goals. Some of these additives have been linked to adverse effects on hormone balance, including potentially lowering testosterone levels. For instance, certain protein shakes contain soy protein isolates, which have been a subject of debate due to their phytoestrogen content—compounds that mimic estrogen in the body. While the scientific community is still exploring the full impact of phytoestrogens on men's hormonal health, there is a growing preference for protein sources that don't carry these uncertainties.

Moreover, the processing involved in creating these protein supplements can strip away valuable nutrients that are naturally found in whole protein sources. This processing can also introduce substances that may contribute to inflammation or disrupt the body's natural hormonal rhythms.

Remember, this journey is not about deprivation; it's about making informed choices. It's about transforming your diet into a powerful tool that not only nourishes your body but also enhances your manhood. As you make these dietary changes, imagine the feeling of power and vitality coursing through your veins. It's a testament to the fact that every meal is an opportunity to fuel not just your body, but your essence as a man.

The Importance of Companionship

In the quest for manhood, and particularly in elevating your testosterone levels and overall well-being, the company you keep plays a pivotal role. This chapter isn't just about friendship; it's about surrounding yourself with like-minded individuals who not only understand your journey but also actively contribute to it. It's about building a tribe that resonates with your values, aspirations, and lifestyle.

Why Your Social Circle Matters

Emotional Support and Motivation: Your friends are your cheerleaders and coaches. They are there to lift you when you're down and push you when you're capable of more. Imagine having a rough day, and there's a friend who reminds you of your strength and resilience. That's the power of supportive companionship.

Shared Interests and Activities:
Engaging in activities with friends who share similar interests, especially in fitness and healthy living, can significantly enhance your commitment to these endeavors. Whether it's a gym buddy or a group that enjoys hiking, these shared experiences not only boost your physical health but also strengthen your bonds.

Positive Influence and Accountability:
Surrounding yourself with people who embody the traits you aspire to can profoundly influence your behavior and decisions. They hold you accountable, not just with words, but through their actions. It's about having friends who practice what they preach, setting a standard that inspires you to do the same.

Learning and Growth:
Like-minded friends often bring different perspectives and knowledge to the table. These interactions are opportunities for learning and

personal growth, helping you expand your understanding of various aspects of life, including fitness, relationships, and personal development.

Cultivating Meaningful Relationships

Seeking Quality over Quantity:
It's not about having a large circle of friends, but having meaningful relationships that add value to your life. Look for depth and authenticity in your connections.

Being Proactive in Building Relationships:
Join groups or communities that align with your interests. Be it a sports team, a fitness class, or an online community, these are avenues to meet like-minded individuals.

Nurturing Existing Relationships:
Invest time and effort in your current relationships. It's about deepening the bonds you already have, providing and receiving support, and growing together.

Setting Boundaries:
Not every social interaction is beneficial. Learn to set boundaries and distance yourself from toxic or negative influences that detract from your goals and well-being.

Being a Good Friend Yourself:
Friendship is a two-way street. Be the kind of friend you wish to have – supportive, honest, and inspiring.

Imagine a life where you're not just striving for betterment in isolation, but are part of a community that uplifts, motivates, and challenges you. This isn't just about individual growth; it's about collective empowerment. Your tribe becomes a reflection of your aspirations, a mirror that not only shows you who you are but also who you can become.

The Importance of Working Out

In the pursuit of manhood, and in the quest to elevate your testosterone levels, working out stands as a cornerstone. This chapter is dedicated to unraveling the comprehensive benefits of regular exercise, not just for your body, but for your mind, your emotions, and your overall quality of life.

Physical Benefits: Beyond Building Muscles

Boosting Testosterone and Overall Health:
Regular exercise, especially strength training and high-intensity workouts, directly boosts testosterone levels, which in turn enhances muscle growth, fat loss, and overall physical health.

Enhanced Energy Levels:
Consistent exercise leads to improved stamina and energy, equipping you to tackle daily tasks with more vigor and enthusiasm.

Longevity and Disease Prevention:
Regular physical activity is key in preventing numerous health issues, including heart disease, diabetes, and certain types of cancer. It's about investing in a longer, healthier life.

Mental and Emotional Gains: The Unseen Rewards

Mental Clarity and Focus:
Exercise is a proven way to clear the mental fog. It enhances cognitive functions, leading to better concentration, creativity, and problem-solving skills.

Stress Relief and Mental Health:
Physical activity is a powerful stress reliever. It releases endorphins, often referred to as 'feel-good' hormones, which can reduce anxiety and depression, promoting a sense of well-being.

Confidence and Self-Esteem:
The discipline and dedication required in maintaining a regular workout routine build inner strength. Every milestone achieved, be it lifting heavier weights or running a longer distance, bolsters your confidence and self-esteem.

Social and Personal Development Aspects

Building Relationships: Gyms, sports clubs, and fitness groups provide opportunities to meet like-minded individuals, fostering both friendship and camaraderie.

Developing Discipline and Resilience:
Adhering to a workout routine develops discipline, a trait that translates to other areas of life, including career and personal relationships.

Enhancing Physical Appearance:
Improved physique as a result of regular exercise can positively affect your self-image and how others perceive you, often leading to better social interactions and opportunities.

Integrating Exercise into Your Life

Finding the Right Activity:
The best workout is one that you enjoy and can stick to consistently. Explore different options - weightlifting, running, swimming, martial arts - and find what resonates with you.

Setting Realistic Goals:
Set achievable goals that motivate you. Whether it's gaining muscle, losing weight, or simply staying active, having clear objectives helps maintain focus and motivation.

Consistency Over Intensity:
It's not about pushing yourself to extremes every single day, but about maintaining a consistent routine. Regular, moderate-intensity workouts are often more sustainable and effective in the long term.

Listening to Your Body:
Pay attention to your body's signals. Rest and recovery are just as important as the workouts themselves.

Imagine a life where you're not just physically stronger but also mentally sharper, emotionally balanced, and socially connected. That's the transformative power of working out. It's a journey that goes far beyond the gym; it's a path to a more fulfilled, vibrant, and powerful you.

Maximizing Testosterone Through Exercise

The link between physical exercise and testosterone is not just a matter of science; it's a key to unlocking a version of yourself that's stronger, more vibrant, and more authentically masculine.

The Testosterone-Boosting Power of Exercise

Understanding the Connection:
Exercise, particularly weight training and high-intensity workouts, stimulates your body to produce more testosterone. It's like igniting the engine of manhood within you.

Targeting Major Muscle Groups:
While all exercise is beneficial, certain types of workouts are particularly effective in boosting testosterone. Focusing on large muscle groups, especially your legs and traps, can lead to significant hormonal surges. Squats, deadlifts, and other compound movements engage these large muscle groups, sending signals to your body to ramp up testosterone production.

The Leg-Testosterone Link:
The legs are one of the largest muscle groups in your body. Working them out doesn't just build strength and endurance; it catalyzes your body's testosterone production. Think of leg days not just as building physical strength, but as forging hormonal resilience.

The Role of Trap Muscles:
Similarly, working on your traps, the muscles around your neck and shoulders, has a significant impact. These muscles are not just for show; they are hormonal powerhouses, responding vigorously to exercise with increased testosterone release.

Personal Stories and Emotional Resonance

Transformative Tales:
Imagine a man who took control of his life by taking control of his fitness. With each squat, each lift, he wasn't just elevating weights; he was elevating his very essence, his testosterone levels, his sense of self.

Overcoming Challenges:
The journey isn't easy. There are days when the weights feel heavier, when your body screams in protest. But it's in these moments of struggle that the real magic happens – both physically and hormonally.

The Emotional High:
There's an undeniable rush, a euphoric high, when you push through a challenging workout. It's more than endorphins; it's a surge of testosterone that leaves you feeling more alive, more masculine.

Incorporating Testosterone-Boosting Workouts Into Your Life

Developing a Routine:
Create a workout schedule that prioritizes compound movements. Incorporate exercises like squats, deadlifts, and overhead presses that work multiple large muscle groups.

Balancing Intensity and Recovery:
While intense workouts boost testosterone, recovery is equally important. Overtraining can lead to fatigue and decreased testosterone levels. Balance is key.

Tracking Progress:
Keep a workout journal. Documenting your progress not only keeps you motivated but also helps you understand the correlation between your workout intensity and how you feel both physically and mentally.

Seeking Professional Guidance:
If you're new to this, consider working with a fitness trainer. They can guide you in developing a workout plan that safely and effectively targets the right muscle groups to maximize testosterone production.

Embrace each workout as an opportunity to not just build muscle, but to fortify your manhood. It's a journey of transformation, where each drop of sweat, each moment of exertion, is a step towards a more potent, vibrant, and powerful version of yourself.

Sculpting Attraction Through Fitness

Beginning a fitness journey is often fueled by the desire for better health, but an equally compelling motivator is the pursuit of physical attractiveness. We delve into the science behind why certain physical traits are universally perceived as attractive and how working out can help you embody these ideals, transforming not just your body but also how you're perceived by others.

The Science of Physical Attraction

Broad Shoulders and a Robust Chest:
Scientific studies have consistently shown that men with broader shoulders and a well-developed chest are often deemed more attractive. These traits are subconsciously associated with strength, health, and genetic fitness – signals that are hardwired into human perception as desirable.

Muscle Definition and Symmetry:
While extreme muscularity is not everyone's goal or ideal, a certain level of muscle definition and body symmetry is universally appealing. It's not just about size; it's about the proportion and harmony of your physical form.

The V-Taper:
This is the classic masculine silhouette – broad shoulders tapering down to a narrower waist. It's a physical embodiment of strength and agility and is perceived as highly attractive in various cultures and societies.

The Confidence Factor:
Imagine looking in the mirror and seeing a transformation not only in your physique but in your self-perception. This physical evolution often leads to a significant boost in confidence, which in itself is an attractive trait.

The Journey of Transformation:
Every individual who embarks on a fitness journey has their story – of struggles, perseverance, and eventual triumph. This narrative of self-improvement and dedication is inherently attractive, reflecting a commitment to personal excellence.

Beyond Aesthetics:
While the pursuit of an attractive physique is a legitimate goal, the process of achieving it often brings about a deeper appreciation for your body, its capabilities, and a sense of gratitude and self-respect.

Incorporating Attractiveness-Focused Workouts into Your Routine

Shoulder and Chest Workouts:
Incorporate exercises like bench presses, push-ups, and overhead presses to build your chest and shoulders. These exercises not only enhance these areas but also contribute to the coveted V-taper.

Whole-Body Symmetry:
Focus on a balanced workout regimen that targets all muscle groups. This ensures proportional muscle development and enhances overall body symmetry.

Body Composition:
Pay attention to your body fat percentage. A leaner physique often highlights muscle definition and contributes to the overall attractiveness of your physical form.

Consistency and Patience:
Building an attractive physique takes time and consistent effort. Set realistic goals and celebrate the small milestones along the way.

The pursuit of an attractive body is more than skin deep. It's a journey that challenges you to push your limits, fosters a deeper connection with your body, and ultimately leads to a transformation that transcends physical appearance. It's about embodying the qualities that you admire, projecting strength, health, and confidence – traits that are universally attractive.

Simple Yet Powerful Tips for Maximum Impact

Beginning a fitness journey is not just about what exercises you do; it's also about how you do them. This part of the book is dedicated to the art of working out efficiently and effectively, offering simple yet scientifically backed tips that can transform your workout experience. These are not just instructions; they are keys to unlocking a more focused, intense, and rewarding training session.

1. The Art of Disconnecting: Leave Your Phone Behind

In our hyper-connected world, your phone can be a constant source of distraction. By leaving it behind, or at least setting it to do not disturb mode, you gift yourself the luxury of focus. This is your time – a sacred slot dedicated to nothing but your physical and mental fortification.

Scientific Insight:

Studies show that minimizing distractions can lead to more focused and effective workouts. Each moment you're not looking at your screen is a moment wholly dedicated to your body's transformation.

2. The Power of Rest: Strategic Pauses Between Sets

Rest intervals are not just pauses; they are an integral part of your training. They allow your muscles to recover briefly, preparing them for the next bout of exertion.

Optimal Rest Periods:

Depending on your goals and the intensity of your exercises, rest periods can vary. For strength training, 1-3 minutes of rest allow for muscular recovery, while shorter rests of 30-60 seconds are ideal for endurance and conditioning.

Science-Backed Approach:
Research suggests that appropriate rest intervals are crucial for maximizing gains in both strength and muscle size. These brief breaks allow for ATP (energy) regeneration in your muscles, making your next set just as powerful as your first.

3. Intensity Over Duration: The 45 to 60 Minute Workout Window
Optimizing workout duration to fit within a 45 to 60-minute window is not only about leveraging hormonal peaks for maximum gains but also about managing your body's energy resources effectively. This strategic timing plays a pivotal role in how your body utilizes fuel, ensuring that your training enhances muscle growth rather than inadvertently leading to muscle loss.

Why Shorter Workouts?:
When engaged in prolonged workouts, especially those extending beyond the 60-minute mark at high intensity, your body starts to deplete its glycogen reserves. Glycogen serves as the primary energy source for your muscles during both aerobic and anaerobic exercise. Once these stores run low, the body seeks alternative energy sources to maintain performance. However, without sufficient glycogen and in the absence of adequate oxygen for fat oxidation, the body faces a conundrum.

The Shift to Protein Catabolism:
In situations where glycogen is scarce and fat cannot be efficiently burned due to a lack of oxygen, the body turns to amino acids from muscle protein as an emergency energy source. This process, known as gluconeogenesis, involves converting proteins into glucose to fuel continued physical effort. Consequently, training excessively, particularly in sessions lasting well beyond an hour, can lead to muscle protein breakdown, undermining your goals for muscle growth and strength.

This counterproductive scenario underscores the importance of not just the intensity but also the duration of workouts. Pushing beyond the glycogen depletion threshold without adequate fuel forces the body into a state where it cannibalizes muscle tissue for energy, counteracting the very essence of strength training and bodybuilding efforts.

The Science:
Empirical studies reinforce that testosterone, the hormone pivotal for muscle growth and recovery, reaches its zenith within this golden window, while cortisol, the stress hormone implicated in muscle catabolism (breakdown), begins to escalate post the one-hour mark of rigorous exercise. Exercising within this optimized timeframe allows athletes and fitness enthusiasts to capitalize on the body's hormonal milieu, enhancing muscle synthesis and minimizing the catabolic effects of cortisol. Additionally, the strategic management of workout duration helps in maintaining glycogen stores, ensuring that muscles are adequately fueled to perform, recover, and grow.

4. Focused Movements and Form

Emphasizing the quality of each repetition over the sheer quantity fundamentally changes the effectiveness of your workout. This principle extends beyond merely avoiding injury; it's about maximizing the engagement and development of targeted muscle groups. Incorporating a focus on muscle contraction and the tempo of your movements can significantly amplify these benefits.

The Importance of Muscle Contraction (The Pump):
Prioritizing the contraction of the muscle during exercises, often referred to as achieving "the pump," is crucial for stimulating muscle growth and strength. This focused contraction ensures that you are not just moving weights but actively engaging and challenging the muscle fibers. The sensation of the muscle being "used" or the pump experienced during and after a workout is not just satisfying; it's indicative of effective muscle engagement and stimulation.

Engaging in exercises with an intention to feel each muscle contract, and ensuring that every movement is deliberate, enhances the mind-muscle connection. This connection is a powerful tool in your training arsenal, as it helps in isolating and targeting muscles more effectively, leading to improved strength and hypertrophy.

The Benefits of Slow Repetitions:
Slowing down your repetitions can exponentially increase the effectiveness of your workout. Performing movements slowly and with control accomplishes several key outcomes:

Increased Time Under Tension:
Slower reps increase the time your muscles are under tension, a critical factor in muscle growth. This sustained tension forces your muscles to work harder, enhancing the stimulus for growth and strengthening.

Enhanced Muscle Activation:
Slow movements ensure better muscle activation by eliminating momentum from the equation. This means the targeted muscle groups do the bulk of the work, leading to more efficient and effective workouts.

Improved Form and Safety:
A slower tempo allows for a greater focus on maintaining proper form throughout the exercise, reducing the risk of injury. It also ensures that the movement is executed through a full range of motion, maximizing the exercise's potential benefits.

Metabolic Stress and Muscle Growth:
Slow repetitions contribute to increased metabolic stress, one of the key mechanisms behind muscle growth. This stress, combined with mechanical tension from lifting, stimulates muscle adaptation and growth at a cellular level.

Incorporating Mindfulness into Movement:
Adopting a mindful approach to your workouts, where you concentrate on the contraction of the muscle and the tempo of your movements, transforms each session into a more effective and meditative practice. It's about being fully present in the moment, connecting with your body, and ensuring that each movement and contraction is performed with intention and focus.

Your Workout, Your Sanctuary
Visualize your workout space as a sanctuary. This is where you shed your daily stresses, focus on your physical and mental strength, and commit to becoming the best version of yourself. Every drop of sweat, every strained breath, is a testament to your dedication and resilience.

As you step into this space, remember these simple yet powerful tips. They are not just strategies; they are rituals that honor your commitment to your body and mind. In the chapters to come, we'll explore how to complement these workouts with nutrition and recovery strategies, ensuring that every aspect of your fitness journey is aligned towards your ultimate goal of health, strength, and vitality.

The Importance of Handling social media

In today's digital age, social media is a landscape that can both enrich and complicate our lives. This chapter isn't just a list of rules; it's a guide to using social media in a way that aligns with the principles of strength, respect, and dignity. It's about being a man who uses these platforms not as a means of escape or validation but as tools for growth, connection, and, when applicable, business.

Understanding the Impact of Social Media on Your Psyche

Before diving into the dos and don'ts, let's acknowledge the elephant in the room: social media can significantly impact your mental health, self-esteem, and perception of reality. The key is to use it consciously and constructively.

The Don'ts: Steering Clear of Pitfalls

Avoid Following Female Models or Provocative Content:
Constant exposure to unrealistic beauty standards and sexually provocative content can distort your perception of relationships and self-worth. It shifts your focus from meaningful life experiences to superficial digital interactions.

Refrain from 'Simp' Comments:
Posting overly flattering or desperate comments on others' posts, especially those of women you don't know, can be perceived as lacking self-respect and confidence. Your words and actions, even online, reflect your character.

Don't Show Off:
While it's tempting to use social media as a highlight reel, constantly boasting about your achievements or lifestyle can come off as insecure and seeking validation. Authenticity is more admirable than bravado.

Avoid Negativity and Toxicity:
Steer clear of engaging in negative or toxic discussions. It's easy to get drawn into the drama, but it serves no purpose and can drain your mental energy.

Don't Let It Consume You:
Spending excessive time on social media can lead to a disconnect from real life, affecting your relationships and real-world experiences. Balance is key.

The Dos: Using Social Media Constructively

Use for Business and Networking:
Social media can be an incredible tool for networking, building your business, and learning. Use it to connect with like-minded individuals, industry leaders, and to keep abreast of trends and opportunities.

Share Positively and Authentically:
When you do post, share content that reflects your genuine interests, achievements, and insights. Let your social media be a reflection of your positive attributes and life philosophy.

Educate and Inspire:
Use your platform to educate, inspire, and spread positivity. Share your journey, the lessons you've learned, and insights that might help others.

Limit Your Usage:
Be mindful of the time you spend on social media. Set specific times for checking these platforms, ensuring it doesn't interfere with your daily productivity and real-life interactions.

Promote Healthy Interactions:
Engage in healthy, constructive conversations. Be respectful, even when you disagree. Your online demeanor should mirror the respectful and dignified person you are offline.

Your Digital Footprint Reflects Your Character

Every action you take on social media is a reflection of your character. As you navigate these digital platforms, ask yourself: Does this align with the man I aspire to be? Use social media not as a crutch for validation but as a stage for positive influence, a tool for growth, and a reflection of the best parts of you.

Remember, the true measure of a man isn't in the likes or followers he has but in the strength of his character, both online and off. In the following chapters, we will explore more aspects of personal development, focusing on building a life that's fulfilling and meaningful, both in the digital world and beyond.

Quick Tips for Navigating Social Media Wisely

Following the insights on handling social media with respect, dignity, and purpose, here are some actionable quick tips to ensure that your digital presence aligns with your values and aspirations:

Consider a Digital Detox:
If social media isn't essential for your personal improvement or business growth, think about taking a break or even deleting platforms like Snapchat, Instagram, Facebook, Twitter, and TikTok. This can reduce distractions and help refocus on real-life connections and goals.

Curate Your Feed for Positivity:
If deleting social media isn't an option, curate your feed. Unfollow accounts that promote unrealistic beauty standards, constant self-promotion, or negativity. Instead, follow accounts that inspire, educate, and resonate with your interests and values.

Cleanse Your Digital Footprint:
Go through your social media accounts and delete any posts, pictures, or videos that seek validation without adding real value to your or others' lives. Cultivate a digital presence that's authentic and reflective of your true self.

End the Cycle of "Simping":
Refrain from engaging in behavior that puts you in a position of over-admiration or desperation, especially in interactions with individuals you don't personally know. Respect yourself and others by fostering interactions that are genuine and respectful.

Avoid the Pitfalls of Online Debates:
Social media is rife with opportunities for endless debates that rarely lead to productive outcomes. Before posting or commenting, consider whether the discussion contributes positively to the conversation or merely fuels unnecessary conflict.

Set Boundaries for Social Media Use:
Establish clear boundaries for when and how long you engage with social media. Designate specific times of the day for checking your feeds, and be mindful not to let it interfere with your work, personal life, or sleep.

Engage in Constructive Conversations:
Use your platform to engage in conversations that promote growth, learning, and positivity. Whether commenting on others' posts or sharing your own content, aim for interactions that reflect the respectful and dignified person you are.

Practice Mindfulness in Your Digital Interactions:
Before posting, liking, or commenting, pause and consider the intent behind your action. Is it to share something meaningful, or is it driven by the desire for external validation? Strive for mindfulness and intentionality in your digital interactions.

Focus on Real-Life Connections:
Use social media as a tool to enhance, not replace, real-life relationships. Make an effort to connect offline with friends, family, and colleagues to build and maintain strong, meaningful relationships.

Reflect on Your Digital Identity:
Regularly take time to reflect on your digital presence. Ask yourself if your social media activity aligns with the person you aspire to be and the life you want to lead. Adjust your habits as necessary to ensure that your digital footprint authentically represents your values and goals.

The Importance of Being busy

In the journey of self-discovery and manhood, being actively engaged in meaningful pursuits – whether it's running a business, cultivating a hobby, or investing in personal projects – is more than a pastime; it's a cornerstone of your identity and self-worth. This chapter delves into why having something you're passionate about is crucial for your mental, emotional, and social well-being.

The Transformative Power of Purposeful Engagement

Distraction from Unproductive Pursuits:
Engaging in meaningful activities shifts your focus from unproductive or obsessive thoughts, particularly about relationships. It channels your energy into something constructive, reducing the likelihood of dwelling on things that don't serve your growth.

Reduced Risk of Depression:
Immersing yourself in projects or businesses provides a sense of accomplishment and progress, key factors in combating feelings of depression and aimlessness. It's about being too engaged in growth and improvement to be bogged down by negative thoughts.

Enhanced Self-Esteem and Confidence:
Building something, be it a business or a skill, fosters a deep sense of achievement. This isn't just about external success; it's about the internal growth that comes from overcoming challenges and reaching milestones.

Attraction Through Ambition and Independence:
Scientific research suggests that individuals who are ambitious and have clear life goals are often perceived as more attractive. This perception stems from the independence, confidence, and resourcefulness that come with pursuing one's passions and goals.

Why Having a Business or Engaging Hobby Matters

Sense of Identity and Fulfillment:
Pursuing a business or a hobby that you're passionate about gives you a sense of identity beyond your social roles. It's about carving out a niche where you feel truly alive and fulfilled.

Building Resilience and Problem-Solving Skills:
The challenges and obstacles inherent in any meaningful pursuit teach resilience and enhance your problem-solving skills, making you more adept at handling life's unpredictabilities.

Social Networking and Relationships:
Engaging in a business or hobby often leads to meeting like-minded individuals, expanding your social network, and building relationships based on mutual interests and respect.

A Platform for Positive Impact:
Your pursuits can become a means of contributing positively to others' lives, whether through your business or by sharing your hobby. It's about creating value that transcends personal gain.

Lifelong Learning and Personal Growth:
The pursuit of a business or hobby is a journey of continuous learning and adaptation. It keeps your mind sharp, your skills fresh, and your life interesting.

Scientific Perspectives on Attraction to Busy Individuals

Perceived Value and Scarcity:
Psychological principles suggest that people are more attracted to things that are perceived as rare or valuable. A man who is busy with meaningful pursuits inherently projects a sense of scarcity and value, making his time and attention more desirable.

Signals of Competence and Ambition:
Evolutionary psychology posits that traits like ambition and competence are attractive because they signal the ability to provide and succeed in various endeavors. A busy man engaged in purposeful activities is seen as competent and ambitious, traits that are subconsciously linked to good partnership qualities.

The Magnetism of Independence:
Independence is a highly attractive trait. Being engaged in personal projects and pursuits signifies a level of independence that suggests confidence and self-sufficiency, qualities that are universally appealing.

Practical Implications: Communication and Availability

In light of these insights, it's clear why not always being immediately available or responsive can enhance your perceived attractiveness. This isn't about playing games or feigning disinterest; it's about genuinely investing your time and energy in passions and pursuits that enrich your life.

Measured Communication:
Waiting to reply to messages isn't about being elusive but respecting your own time and commitments. It communicates that you lead a full, engaging life outside of your social interactions.

Genuine Unavailability:
True unavailability stems from a life rich with activities and commitments. It's not a tactic but a natural consequence of living a purpose-driven life. This authenticity is what truly enhances your attractiveness, as it's rooted in genuine self-improvement and fulfillment.

Broadening the Benefits: Beyond Attraction

Embracing a busy life filled with purposeful engagement extends benefits far beyond increasing your attractiveness:

Self-Actualization:
Pursuing your passions leads to a more fulfilled and content life, aligning with Maslow's hierarchy of needs towards self-actualization.

Enhanced Cognitive Function:
Engaging in challenging activities and learning new skills keeps the brain active and healthy, contributing to better cognitive function over time.

Improved Social Skills:
Being involved in various activities naturally enhances your social network and skills, making you more adept in interpersonal interactions.

Contributing to a Legacy:
Investing in meaningful work and hobbies allows you to contribute positively to the world, leaving a legacy that transcends personal success.

Finding Your Passion

The key to reaping the benefits of being busy lies in finding something that genuinely excites and challenges you. It's not about being busy for the sake of it; it's about being invested in something that resonates with your deepest interests and values.

As you embark on this path, remember, it's not just about what you're doing; it's about who you're becoming in the process. A man with purpose and passion is a man who commands respect and admiration, not just from others, but from himself.

The Importance of Conquering Fears

Facing and overcoming fears is a crucial aspect of personal growth and development. This chapter is dedicated to identifying common fears that many individuals face and providing science-backed strategies for overcoming them. By confronting our fears, we not only gain courage but also open doors to new experiences and a fuller life.

Understanding and Overcoming Common Fears

Fear of Failure (Atychiphobia):
Origin: Often rooted in perfectionism and a desire for approval.

Overcoming Strategy: Embrace failure as a learning opportunity. Set realistic goals and celebrate small successes. Cognitive Behavioral Therapy (CBT) is scientifically proven to help in redefining one's perception of failure and success.

Fear of Rejection (Anthropophobia):
Origin: Linked to social anxiety and past experiences of rejection.
Overcoming Strategy: Practice self-affirmation and build self-esteem. Exposure therapy, gradually increasing social interactions, can reduce the intensity of this fear.

Fear of Change (Metathesiophobia):
Origin: Stemming from a desire for stability and predictability.
Overcoming Strategy: Start with small changes to build adaptability. Mindfulness and stress-reduction techniques can help in accepting and embracing change.

Fear of Loneliness (Autophobia):
Origin: Can be related to low self-esteem and lack of self-reliance.
Overcoming Strategy: Engage in activities that foster self-discovery and self-sufficiency. Building a strong support network and participating in community activities can also mitigate this fear.

Fear of Success (Achievemephobia):
Origin: Paradoxically linked to fear of change and added responsibilities.
Overcoming Strategy: Define personal definitions of success. Break down goals into manageable steps and focus on the journey rather than just the outcome.

Fear of Intimacy (Aphenphosmphobia):
Origin: Often associated with past trauma or negative relationship experiences.
Overcoming Strategy: Therapy, especially focused on past trauma, can be highly effective. Building trust gradually in relationships and communicating openly about fears can also help.

Fear of Heights (Acrophobia):
Origin: Related to a natural sense of danger and self-preservation.
Overcoming Strategy: Gradual exposure under controlled conditions can reduce anxiety. Virtual reality therapy has shown promising results in treating acrophobia.

Fear of Public Speaking (Glossophobia):
Origin: Tied to social anxiety and fear of embarrassment.
Overcoming Strategy: Practice and preparation are key. Joining groups like Toastmasters can provide a supportive environment to improve public speaking skills.

The Science of Fear Management

Exposure Therapy: Gradually and repeatedly exposing oneself to the fear source in a controlled way is a well-established method to reduce fear.

Cognitive Behavioral Therapy (CBT):
Helps in identifying and changing negative thought patterns associated with the fear.

Mindfulness and Relaxation Techniques:
These practices can reduce anxiety and stress, making it easier to face fears.

Fear Makes the Wolf Seem Bigger Than He Is

The adage "**Fear makes the wolf seem bigger than he is**" serves as a potent metaphor for the nature of fear and its impact on our perception of challenges. This saying encapsulates the idea that our fears, when left unchecked, can distort our perception of reality, making obstacles appear more daunting than they truly are.

The Psychological Mechanism Behind the Adage
Scientific studies in cognitive psychology reveal that fear can amplify the perceived difficulty or danger of a situation. This distortion is rooted in our brain's response to potential threats. The amygdala, a key part of the brain involved in processing emotions, becomes activated in the presence of fear, heightening our emotional response and potentially skewing our rational assessment of the situation. This heightened state can lead to an exaggerated perception of threat or challenge, much like seeing the wolf as larger and more menacing than it actually is.

Applying Science to Shrink the Wolf

Cognitive Reframing: Cognitive Behavioral Therapy (CBT) offers tools for cognitive reframing, enabling individuals to challenge and alter irrational fears. By questioning the validity of the exaggerated perceptions fueled by fear, one can reduce the 'size' of the 'wolf,' seeing challenges more realistically.

Exposure Therapy:
This technique involves gradual and controlled exposure to the source of fear, which can help diminish the exaggerated perception of danger. Over time, as the fear response decreases, the 'wolf' shrinks back to its

actual size, revealing that the obstacle or threat was manageable all along.

Mindfulness and Relaxation Techniques:
Practices such as mindfulness meditation and deep breathing exercises can help calm the amygdala, reducing the emotional intensity associated with fear. By adopting a more relaxed and present state of mind, individuals can perceive challenges with greater clarity and less distortion.

Embracing the Journey Beyond Fear
Understanding that "fear makes the wolf seem bigger than he is" encourages a shift in perspective. It invites us to confront our fears not as insurmountable beasts but as manageable challenges that we have the power to overcome. This realization is empowering, transforming fear from a barrier into a catalyst for growth, resilience, and self-discovery.

The Courage to Face Fear

Facing our fears is not just a battle against external challenges; it's an inward journey of discovering our courage and strength. It's about not letting fear dictate our choices and embracing life's opportunities fully.

Remember, every step taken to confront and overcome fear is a step towards personal empowerment and freedom. The journey might be challenging, but it's a path that leads to resilience, confidence, and a richer life experience.

The Importance of Self-Confidence

Self-confidence is a cornerstone of success and fulfillment in life. This chapter delves into the various causes of low self-confidence and provides practical, science-backed strategies for building and nurturing this essential trait. The journey to self-confidence is deeply personal and transformative, leading not just to external success but to inner peace and contentment.

Root Causes of Low Self-Confidence

Negative Past Experiences:
Traumatic or negative experiences, especially during formative years, can significantly impact self-esteem.
Solution: Therapy, particularly Cognitive Behavioral Therapy (CBT), can help process and overcome these past experiences. Building new, positive experiences can also reshape self-perception.

Unrealistic Social Comparisons:
Comparing oneself to others, especially in the age of social media, can lead to feelings of inadequacy.
Solution: Focus on your own personal growth and achievements. Practice gratitude and don't compare yourself to others.

Fear of Failure:
The fear of not meeting expectations, whether one's own or others', can paralyze action and erode confidence.
Solution: Embrace a growth mindset, where failure is seen as a learning opportunity rather than a defeat.

Negative Self-Talk:
Constantly belittling oneself and doubting one's abilities perpetuates low self-esteem.
Solution: Practice positive self-talk and affirmations. Challenge and replace negative thoughts with constructive ones.

Lack of Goal-Setting:
Without clear goals, it's easy to feel adrift and doubt one's abilities and purpose.
Solution: Set specific, achievable goals and work towards them. Celebrate small successes along the way.

Physical Health Issues:
Poor physical health, lack of exercise, or neglecting personal appearance can negatively affect self-confidence.
Solution: Engage in regular physical activity, eat a balanced diet, and take care of your physical appearance.

Testosterone

Testosterone is often associated with traits traditionally deemed masculine, such as assertiveness, competitiveness, and self-assurance. Scientific studies have shown that optimal levels of this hormone are linked to increased self-confidence. This connection is not merely about physical prowess but extends to a psychological state of being that influences how individuals perceive themselves and interact with the world.

Confidence and Assertiveness:
Higher testosterone levels are correlated with a greater sense of assertiveness and a lower likelihood of experiencing social anxiety. This hormonal influence can enhance one's willingness to take risks and assert oneself in social and professional settings.

Emotional Regulation:
Testosterone plays a role in modulating emotional responses. While excessive levels can impede empathy and emotional understanding, balanced testosterone levels support emotional strength and resilience, aiding in the processing and regulation of emotions.

Addressing the Lack of Testosterone

For those experiencing low self-confidence, particularly men, a deficiency in testosterone might be a contributing factor. This deficiency can manifest not only in diminished confidence but also in challenges with processing emotions effectively.

Solution for Hormonal Balance:

Seeking medical advice to assess testosterone levels can be a starting point. For some, hormone replacement therapy (HRT) or lifestyle changes such as improved diet, regular exercise, and stress management techniques can help in balancing testosterone levels, thereby positively influencing self-confidence and emotional well-being.

Enhancing Emotional Processing Through Lifestyle Adjustments

In addition to potential medical interventions, focusing on lifestyle adjustments that naturally enhance testosterone levels—and by extension, self-confidence and emotional regulation—can be beneficial:

Regular Physical Activity:

Engaging in strength training and cardiovascular exercises can naturally boost testosterone levels, improving mood and confidence.

Nutrition:

Consuming a balanced diet rich in proteins, healthy fats, and certain minerals like zinc and vitamin D can support testosterone production.

Stress Reduction:

Since stress elevates cortisol levels, which in turn can suppress testosterone production, adopting stress-reduction techniques such as mindfulness, meditation, or yoga can be instrumental in maintaining hormonal balance.

Scientific Insights into Building Self-Confidence

Neuroplasticity and Confidence:
The brain's ability to change (neuroplasticity) means that confidence can be developed and strengthened over time through practice and positive experiences.

The Role of Endorphins:
Physical activity releases endorphins, which have mood-boosting properties that can enhance self-esteem.

Goal-Setting Theory:
Psychological research shows that setting and achieving goals can lead to increased self-efficacy and confidence.

Emotional Journey to Self-Confidence

Building self-confidence is more than changing external behaviors; it's about beginning an emotional journey that involves self-discovery, self-acceptance, and self-love. It's about recognizing your intrinsic worth and embracing your unique qualities and strengths.

Remember, the path to self-confidence is not linear; it's filled with ups and downs. Each step forward, no matter how small, is a step toward a more confident and empowered you.

The Importance of Masculinity

In a world where the concept of masculinity is often debated and sometimes misunderstood, it's essential to recognize and embrace the positive aspects of masculinity. This chapter explores the importance of healthy masculinity, how it can be a force for good, and why it's something to be proud of, not ashamed. We delve into the scientific, psychological, and social perspectives that underscore the value of masculinity, addressing the emotional journey involved in embracing it fully.

The Positive Aspects of Healthy Masculinity

Leadership and Responsibility:
Traditional masculine traits like leadership, decisiveness, and a sense of responsibility can be powerful forces for positive change in both personal and professional realms.

Protective and Providing Qualities:
The instinct to protect and provide for one's family and community is a facet of masculinity that has been valued across cultures and time.

Resilience and Strength:
Masculinity is often associated with physical and emotional strength, resilience, and the ability to face challenges head-on.

Courage and Assertiveness:
Being assertive and courageous in standing up for what is right and pursuing goals is a positive masculine trait.

Rationality and Problem-Solving:
The ability to approach problems logically and find solutions is another aspect of traditional masculinity that contributes positively to various aspects of life.

Scientific Insights into the Benefits of Masculinity

Psychological Studies:
Research has shown that certain masculine traits, such as assertiveness and leadership, are linked to higher self-esteem and life satisfaction.

Sociological Perspectives:
Societies have historically valued masculine traits like strength and protectiveness, as they often contribute to the stability and safety of communities.

Biological Aspects:
Testosterone, the hormone most associated with masculinity, has been linked to traits like competitiveness and risk-taking, which can be advantageous in various situations.

The Attraction to Masculinity

Evolutionary Psychology:
From an evolutionary standpoint, certain masculine traits are often seen as attractive because they are subconsciously associated with health, vitality, and the ability to provide and protect.

Social Studies:
Surveys and studies have shown that many people are attracted to confidence, strength, and decisiveness – traits often associated with traditional masculinity.

Navigating the Modern Landscape of Masculinity

In the discourse on masculinity, distinguishing between toxic and healthy expressions of masculinity is paramount. An essential clarification is needed regarding the concept of toxic masculinity, which, paradoxically, can be viewed as a manifestation of non-masculine traits. This perspective arises from the observation that behaviors often labeled as "toxic" – such as aggression, emotional instability, and the inability to process emotions healthily – are antithetical to the core strengths of true masculinity.

Reframing Toxic Masculinity

Toxic masculinity is often characterized by a display of instability and impulsiveness, where individuals react aggressively or defensively in situations that challenge their self-perception or evoke strong emotions. This reactive stance is less about the expression of authentic masculinity and more about the lack of emotional maturity and self-control. Healthy masculinity, in contrast, involves the capacity to experience emotions fully while also exercising discernment in how those emotions are expressed and managed.

The Misconception of Emotional Expression

A critical aspect of redefining masculinity involves dismantling the misconception that emotional expression is inherently unmasculine. On the contrary, the ability to understand, control, and appropriately express emotions is a hallmark of maturity and strength. It is a misinterpretation to view the unregulated outburst of emotions, often seen in toxic masculinity, as a masculine trait. True strength is found in the ability to be vulnerable without being overwhelmed, to be passionate without being reckless, and to be assertive without being oppressive.

Healthy Masculinity and Emotional Control

Healthy masculinity champions emotional resilience and intelligence. It encourages men to acknowledge their emotions, understand their origins, and make informed decisions on how to act on them, rather than being led by fleeting emotional impulses. This level of emotional control is not about suppression but about management and understanding, ensuring that actions are guided by wisdom and consideration.

Cultivating a Balanced Masculinity

The journey towards a balanced and healthy masculinity is one of continuous self-reflection, learning, and growth. It involves:

Embracing Vulnerability:
Seeing vulnerability as a strength that fosters genuine connections with others and encourages personal growth.

Practicing Emotional Intelligence:
Developing the skills to recognize, understand, and manage one's emotions and the emotions of others.

Exercising Compassion and Empathy:
Engaging with the world from a place of understanding and compassion, valuing others' experiences and perspectives.

Promoting Equality and Respect:
Upholding principles of equality and respect in all interactions, recognizing the inherent worth of every individual.

Conclusion

In navigating the modern landscape of masculinity, it is crucial to embrace an authentic expression that values emotional intelligence, respect, and personal integrity. Healthy masculinity is about being the best version of oneself, contributing positively to society, and engaging in relationships with kindness, understanding, and strength. By redefining masculinity in this way, we celebrate a form that enriches not just the individual but the wider community, marking a departure from toxic traits and moving towards a more inclusive and empowering understanding of what it means to be masculine.

The Importance of Loyalty

Loyalty, a trait revered across cultures and time, is more than a moral virtue; it's a foundational element of character and relationships. This chapter explores the importance of loyalty in various aspects of life, including personal relationships, professional environments, and self-identity. We delve into the scientific underpinnings that highlight the benefits of loyalty and how it enriches both the individual who practices it and those who receive it.

Understanding Loyalty and Its Importance

Loyalty in Relationships:
At the heart of any strong relationship is the principle of loyalty. It fosters trust, security, and a deep sense of belonging, essential for any lasting bond.

Loyalty in Professional Life:
In a professional context, loyalty contributes to a sense of team cohesion and organizational commitment, often leading to greater job satisfaction and productivity.

Loyalty to Oneself:
Personal loyalty involves staying true to one's values and beliefs. It's about integrity and consistency in one's actions and decisions.

Scientific Insights into Loyalty

Psychological Benefits:
Studies in psychology have shown that loyalty in relationships leads to higher levels of trust, emotional security, and relationship satisfaction.

Impact on Mental Health:
Loyalty can contribute to better mental health outcomes. The stability and security it brings to relationships act as buffers against stress and anxiety.

Loyalty in Social Groups:
Anthropological research highlights the role of loyalty in social cohesion and group survival, underscoring its evolutionary benefits.

The Emotional Depth of Loyalty

A Sense of Belonging:
Loyalty provides a sense of belonging and connection, fundamental human needs. It's about being part of something larger than oneself.

Resilience in Adversity:
Loyal bonds often prove their strength in times of adversity. Standing by someone through thick and thin builds a deeper, more resilient connection.

The Reward of Reciprocity:
Loyalty is often reciprocated, creating a cycle of trust and support that strengthens relationships.

Navigating Loyalty in the Modern World

In a world where options are plentiful and commitments can be fleeting, loyalty becomes an even more precious commodity. It's about making choices that align with your values and standing by them.

Loyalty as a Personal Commitment

Embracing loyalty is a commitment to oneself and others. It's a conscious choice to prioritize and nurture the relationships and values that matter most. This commitment, while sometimes challenging, is immensely rewarding.

Loyalty's Role in Personal Growth

Loyalty also plays a significant role in personal growth. It teaches patience, understanding, and the value of long-term perspectives. It challenges you to be a better person, partner, friend, and professional.

Remember, loyalty is not about blind allegiance or self-sacrifice. It's about choosing where and with whom to invest your trust, energy, and commitment. It's about the strength of character and the richness it brings to your life and the lives of those around you.

The Importance of Stoicism

In the pursuit of personal growth and understanding, the ancient philosophy of Stoicism offers timeless wisdom that is remarkably applicable to modern life. Stoicism teaches the value of understanding what is within our control and what is not, encouraging a life of virtue, wisdom, and emotional resilience. This chapter explores the importance of Stoicism, backed by scientific insights, and delves into how adopting its principles can profoundly impact your well-being, relationships, and perspective on life.

The Foundations of Stoicism

Stoicism, founded in the Hellenistic period in Greece, is more than just enduring pain or hardship without complaint; it's about recognizing the power of the human mind to cultivate peace, happiness, and understanding, regardless of external circumstances.

Why Stoicism Is Beneficial

Emotional Regulation:
Stoicism teaches the practice of regulating emotions through rational thought, leading to greater emotional stability and resilience.

Focus on What Can Be Controlled:
By emphasizing the importance of focusing on what is within our control, Stoicism encourages proactive engagement with life's challenges, enhancing feelings of empowerment and efficacy.

Resilience in the Face of Adversity:
The stoic practice of preparing for and accepting adversity reduces the impact of negative events, fostering a robust psychological resilience.

Improved Relationships:
Stoicism promotes understanding and empathy, reducing conflict and enhancing the quality of personal and professional relationships.

Clarity of Thought and Purpose:
The stoic emphasis on living according to nature and reason leads to a clearer sense of purpose and direction in life.

Scientific Insights into Stoicism

Cognitive Behavioral Therapy (CBT):
Modern CBT is rooted in Stoic philosophy, particularly in its approach to challenging and changing unhelpful thoughts and behaviors, demonstrating the effectiveness of stoic practices in mental health treatment.

Neuroscience and Emotional Regulation:
Studies in neuroscience have shown that techniques similar to those used in Stoicism can change the brain's response to stress, reducing reactivity to negative emotional stimuli.

Psychological Well-Being:
Research has linked practices similar to Stoic principles, such as mindfulness and acceptance, with higher levels of psychological well-being and lower levels of depression and anxiety.

The Personal Journey of Adopting Stoicism

Embracing Stoicism is not about suppressing emotions or enduring hardship silently; it's about cultivating a profound inner strength that allows you to face life's challenges with grace and wisdom. It's a journey towards understanding the true nature of happiness and learning how to achieve it through virtue, reason, and self-control.

Stoicism in Everyday Life

Incorporating stoic principles into your life can transform the way you perceive and interact with the world. Imagine facing adversity not as a barrier but as an opportunity for growth, engaging with others not with judgment but with empathy, and approaching each day not as a series of obstacles but as a path to wisdom.

Stoicism and Modern Masculinity

For men seeking a model of strength that is not predicated on physical might or dominance, Stoicism offers an alternative: the strength of character, integrity, and intellectual and emotional fortitude. It's a vision of masculinity that values self-mastery, responsibility, and respect for others.

Conclusion: Stoicism as a Way of Life

Adopting Stoicism is about more than embracing a set of philosophical principles; it's about choosing a way of life that emphasizes personal responsibility, emotional resilience, and the pursuit of virtue. It's a pathway to a life lived with intention, wisdom, and profound inner peace.

The Importance of Purpose

Discovering and embracing a personal purpose is one of the most transformative journeys an individual can undertake. This chapter delves into the profound significance of having a purpose, supported by scientific evidence, and explores how it shapes our identity, fuels our motivation, and imbues our lives with meaning. Purpose is not just a philosophical concept but a practical guidepost that enhances well-being, resilience, and fulfillment.

The Essence of Purpose

Purpose can be understood as a sense of direction that aligns with one's values, passions, and strengths, contributing to something greater than oneself. It's the "why" that drives us, the compass that guides our decisions, actions, and aspirations.

Why Purpose Is Crucial

Enhanced Well-being and Life Satisfaction:
Research consistently shows that individuals with a clear sense of purpose experience higher levels of happiness, life satisfaction, and mental well-being.

Resilience Against Stress and Adversity:
Having a purpose provides a buffer against the challenges and stresses of life, offering a sense of stability and perspective that fosters resilience.

Longevity and Health Benefits:
Studies have found that individuals with a strong sense of purpose tend to live longer and have a lower risk of heart disease, stroke, and depression.

Increased Productivity and Achievement:
Purpose fuels motivation and dedication, leading to greater engagement, productivity, and success in personal and professional endeavors.

Improved Social Relationships:
A sense of purpose often involves contributions to the community or meaningful social connections, leading to richer, more fulfilling relationships.

Scientific Insights into the Power of Purpose

Neuroscience:
Brain imaging studies suggest that purposeful living is associated with positive neural patterns related to reward and satisfaction, enhancing overall mental health.

Psychology:
Psychological research links purpose to improved coping strategies, reduced impact of stress, and enhanced self-esteem, underscoring its role in emotional well-being.

Epidemiology:
Epidemiological studies have found correlations between a sense of purpose and reduced mortality rates, highlighting the health benefits of purposeful living.

Cultivating Your Purpose

Finding and embracing your purpose is a personal and often evolving journey. It involves introspection, exploring your values and passions, and considering how you can contribute meaningfully to the world around you.

Self-reflection:
Spend time reflecting on what truly matters to you, what you are passionate about, and where you find deep satisfaction.

Explore and Experiment:
Engage in various activities and pursuits to discover what resonates with your core values and interests.

Set Goals:
Translate your sense of purpose into actionable goals and steps, allowing you to make concrete progress towards your aspirations.

Seek Feedback:
Engage with mentors, peers, or coaches who can provide insight and feedback on your journey towards purposeful living.

The Journey to Purpose

Embracing a purpose is an emotional journey that challenges us to grow, confront our fears, and ultimately find a sense of fulfillment and peace. It's about creating a life that feels authentically yours, one that is driven by your deepest values and aspirations.

Living with Purpose

Living with purpose is about more than finding direction; it's about crafting a life filled with passion, meaning, and contribution. It's a journey that enriches every aspect of your existence, offering a profound sense of fulfillment and joy that comes from knowing you are living in alignment with your true self.

The Importance of Self-Care

In the journey toward self-improvement and personal growth, self-care emerges as a fundamental practice. This chapter delves into the holistic concept of self-care, encompassing physical, emotional, and mental well-being. Self-care is more than an act of indulgence; it's a necessary discipline that fuels our ability to lead, inspire, and care for others. By integrating scientific insights, this discussion will highlight the profound benefits of self-care, from grooming rituals like taking care of your hair and skin to the deeper aspects of mental and emotional health.

The Benefits of Self-Care

Physical Health and Appearance:
Regular self-care routines, including grooming, exercise, and nutrition, significantly impact physical health and appearance. These practices not only enhance personal appearance but also contribute to overall health and longevity.

Self-Esteem and Confidence:
Engaging in self-care routines reinforces self-worth and boosts confidence. This positive self-perception impacts every aspect of life, from personal relationships to professional success.

Resilience and Stress Management:
Effective self-care strategies enhance resilience, enabling individuals to manage stress more effectively and maintain emotional equilibrium in the face of challenges.

Scientific Insights into Self-Care

Neurological Benefits:
Research in neuroscience has shown that self-care activities can stimulate the production of feel-good neurotransmitters, such as serotonin and dopamine, which enhance mood and well-being.

Psychological Impact:
Psychological studies link self-care practices with reduced levels of cortisol, a stress hormone, thereby lowering stress and improving quality of life.

Dermatological Health:
Dermatological research underscores the importance of skin care, not only for aesthetic reasons but also for its protective functions, preventing issues like skin cancer and other disorders.

Cultivating a Self-Care Routine

Personal Grooming:
Regular grooming rituals, such as hair care, skin care, and personal hygiene, are essential components of self-care. They not only improve appearance but also foster a sense of discipline and self-respect.

Nutrition:
A balanced diet nourishes the body, supports mental health, and boosts energy levels, enabling individuals to tackle daily challenges more effectively.

Outdoor Adventures:
Exploring the great outdoors through activities like hiking, camping, or fishing can be a powerful way to connect with nature, challenge oneself, and find tranquility away from the hustle and bustle of daily life.

Skill Development:
Learning new skills or honing existing ones, such as woodworking, mechanical repairs, or playing a musical instrument, not only enriches life with new hobbies but also enhances self-esteem and cognitive function.

Social Connections:
Building and maintaining strong relationships with friends and family is vital for emotional support and can significantly contribute to overall well-being.

Financial Health:
Taking control of financial matters, budgeting wisely, and planning for the future can alleviate stress and contribute to a sense of security and self-sufficiency.

Rest and Recovery:
Ensuring adequate rest, including quality sleep and relaxation techniques, is essential for physical recovery, mental clarity, and emotional resilience.

Time Management:
Effective time management allows for a balanced lifestyle, ensuring that there's space for both responsibilities and leisure, leading to a more fulfilling and less stressful life.

Goal Setting:
Setting realistic and achievable goals provides direction, motivates progress, and gives a sense of accomplishment that boosts confidence and satisfaction.

Adventure Sports:
Participating in adventure sports or physical challenges, such as martial arts, rock climbing, or marathon running, promotes physical fitness, mental toughness, and the spirit of adventure.

Culinary Skills:
Developing culinary skills not only enhances the ability to nourish oneself with healthy, homemade meals but also offers a creative outlet and a way to share with others.

Travel:
Exploring new cultures and destinations broadens horizons, offers new perspectives, and can be a profound way to learn more about oneself and the world.

Emotional Journey of Self-Care

Adopting a self-care regimen is an act of self-love and respect. It's about acknowledging your worth and investing in your well-being. The emotional journey of self-care is deeply personal, reflecting a commitment to nurturing oneself in order to thrive.

The Essential Role of Self-Care

Self-care is the bedrock upon which personal success and fulfillment rest. It's a testament to the belief that taking care of oneself is not selfish but necessary. This chapter invites you to embrace self-care as a vital practice for enhancing your quality of life, empowering you to become the best version of yourself.

The Importance of Being Alone

In a world that often equates being alone with loneliness, there's profound strength and wisdom to be found in solitude. This chapter explores the invaluable benefits of spending time alone, a practice that fosters self-reflection, growth, and emotional resilience. "**There's a difference between being alone and feeling alone.**" This distinction is crucial in understanding how solitude can be a deeply enriching, rather than isolating, experience.

The Science of Solitude

Recent studies in psychology and neuroscience have begun to unveil the benefits of solitude. It's been shown that spending time alone, when embraced willingly, can lead to increased creativity, improved mental health, and enhanced self-understanding.

Enhanced Creativity and Problem-Solving:
Solitude provides a unique environment for the mind to wander freely, fostering creativity and innovation. Studies suggest that individuals often come up with their most creative ideas when they are alone, free from the distractions and influences of others.

Improved Mental Health:
While chronic isolation can be detrimental, intentional solitude has been linked to reduced stress, lower levels of depression, and increased life satisfaction. Time spent alone allows for emotional processing and self-reflection, contributing to a more stable and positive emotional state.

Increased Self-Understanding and Emotional Intelligence:
Solitude forces an inward journey, an opportunity to confront and understand one's thoughts, feelings, and desires. This self-awareness is a cornerstone of emotional intelligence, enhancing one's ability to navigate social relationships more effectively.

The Benefits of Choosing Solitude

Choosing to spend time alone can be a powerful decision. It allows for a deepened sense of self, clarity of purpose, and an enhanced capacity for resilience.

Building a Stronger Mindset:
Alone time is fertile ground for developing a stronger, more independent mindset. It challenges you to find contentment and validation from within, rather than seeking it from external sources.

Cultivating Mindfulness and Presence:
Solitude encourages mindfulness. In silence and stillness, one can better tune into the present moment, appreciating the subtleties of life that are often overlooked in the hustle of social interactions.

Fostering Independence and Self-sufficiency:
Regular periods of solitude can foster a sense of independence, teaching you to be self-sufficient and content with your own company. This independence is liberating, reducing the fear of loneliness and empowering you to choose relationships that genuinely add value to your life.

Enhancing Creativity:
Solitude serves as a catalyst for creativity. The quiet and peace that come with being alone provide the perfect environment for the mind to wander, explore, and create without distractions. Historical figures and creative minds have often cited solitude as a significant factor in their ability to produce groundbreaking work. Scientific studies support this, showing that time spent in solitude can enhance problem-solving skills and artistic expression.

Improving Concentration and Productivity:
In a world brimming with constant noise and interruptions, solitude offers a sanctuary for deep focus and heightened productivity. The

absence of distractions allows for more efficient work and study, leading to higher quality outcomes and a greater sense of achievement.

Strengthening Decision-Making Skills:
Solitude provides the space to reflect on one's values, goals, and the various options before making decisions. This introspection leads to more authentic and well-considered choices, aligned with one's true self rather than being influenced by the opinions and expectations of others.

Facilitating Emotional Healing:
Spending time alone, especially in nature or in quiet reflection, can have therapeutic effects on emotional well-being. It allows for the processing and understanding of emotions, facilitating healing after stressful events or emotional upheavals. Psychological research suggests that solitude can reduce stress levels and lower the risk of mental health disorders.

Deepening Self-Knowledge:
Perhaps one of the most significant benefits of solitude is the opportunity it provides for self-discovery. In the silence of solitude, you are confronted with your true self, stripped of societal masks and pressures. This can lead to profound insights into your personality, desires, and areas of life that need attention or change.

Encouraging Self-Care:
Solitude allows for undistracted attention to self-care practices, whether that's engaging in a hobby, reading, exercising, or simply resting. This dedicated time for self-care is essential for maintaining physical, emotional, and mental health.

Navigating the Path to Solitude

Embracing solitude requires intentional practice. It's about finding balance and recognizing that solitude is not about cutting yourself off from the world but about enriching your inner life to enhance your engagements with the world.

Start Small:
Begin with short periods of solitude, gradually increasing the time as you become more comfortable with your own company.

Create a Solitude Ritual:
Establish a routine or activity that you enjoy doing alone, whether it's journaling, meditating, hiking, or simply sitting quietly with your thoughts.

Reflect and Recharge:
Use your time alone to reflect on your goals, values, and emotions. This practice can recharge your emotional batteries, giving you more energy and enthusiasm for your social interactions.

Conclusion: Solitude as a Source of Strength

Solitude, when embraced willingly and thoughtfully, is not a state to be avoided but a profound source of strength, creativity, and self-discovery. It teaches you to be comfortable in your own skin, to find peace and contentment from within, and to cultivate a life that is true to your values and aspirations.

The Importance of Hardship

In the journey of life, hardship and pain are often viewed through a lens of adversity, something to be avoided or feared. Yet, it is through these very experiences of hardship that individuals, especially men, forge their character, resilience, and depth. This chapter explores the transformative power of hardship, illustrating why enduring and overcoming difficulties is not just beneficial but essential for personal growth and the cultivation of a robust, compassionate, and resilient man.

The Role of Hardship in Personal Development

Hardship, in its many forms—whether physical, emotional, or mental—presents a unique opportunity for growth. It acts as a crucible, testing and refining an individual's character, revealing strengths previously unrecognized and highlighting areas in need of development.

Building Resilience:
Psychological research consistently shows that overcoming adversity strengthens resilience, the ability to bounce back from setbacks. Each challenge faced and navigated enhances one's capacity to handle future difficulties, fostering a sense of self-efficacy and inner fortitude.

Cultivating Empathy and Compassion:
Experiencing hardship can deepen one's empathy and compassion for others. Understanding pain on a personal level can broaden one's perspective, fostering a more profound connection to the struggles of others and enhancing interpersonal relationships.

Forging Mental Toughness:
The process of facing and overcoming hardship is instrumental in developing mental toughness. This quality, characterized by

determination, focus, confidence, and the ability to maintain control under pressure, is crucial for success in all life's arenas.

Enhancing Problem-Solving Skills:
Navigating through difficult times requires creativity and adaptability in problem-solving. These experiences sharpen one's ability to think critically and innovatively, valuable skills in both personal and professional contexts.

Promoting Personal Growth:
Hardship forces an individual to confront their limits, often leading to personal growth. The process of overcoming obstacles can lead to a reevaluation of priorities, a deeper understanding of one's values, and a reinvigorated sense of purpose.

Scientific Insights into the Benefits of Hardship

Neuroscience and psychology offer insights into how hardship contributes to personal development:

Neuroplasticity:
Facing challenges and learning from them can lead to neuroplastic changes in the brain, enhancing cognitive abilities and emotional regulation.

Stress Inoculation:
Similar to a vaccine, experiencing manageable levels of stress can "inoculate" the individual against future stressors, improving stress response and reducing vulnerability to anxiety and depression.

Psychological Theories of Growth:
Concepts such as post-traumatic growth highlight how individuals can derive meaning, strength, and an increased sense of personal worth from overcoming adversity.

Embracing Hardship with Purpose and Perspective

While acknowledging the value of hardship, it's crucial to approach challenges with the right mindset:

Viewing Hardship as an Opportunity:
Reframing adversity as an opportunity for growth can transform one's experience of it, shifting from victimhood to agency.

Seeking Support When Needed:
Recognizing when to seek support is a strength, not a weakness. Sharing burdens and learning from others' wisdom are integral to navigating hardship effectively.

Maintaining Balance:
While embracing hardship, it's important to balance challenges with periods of rest and recovery, ensuring that stress does not become overwhelming or chronic.

Conclusion: Hardship as a Pathway to Excellence

Hardship is not merely an obstacle to be endured but a pathway to personal excellence. It molds character, hones virtues, and unveils potential. For men seeking to embody the best of masculinity, embracing hardship with courage, wisdom, and an open heart is a testament to their commitment to growth, leadership, and a life lived fully.

Through the lens of hardship, we are offered the chance to redefine what it means to be strong, not just in the face of adversity but in the pursuit of a life marked by depth, compassion, and resilience. In this way, hardship becomes not just a teacher but a trusted guide on the path to becoming a good man.

The Importance of Taking Risks

In the quest for personal and professional fulfillment, taking risks stands as a pivotal chapter in the narrative of manhood. This chapter delves into the essence of risk-taking, exploring why stepping beyond the familiar bounds of the comfort zone is not just advisable but essential for achieving greatness. Through the lens of science and personal growth, we uncover the profound impact of embracing uncertainty and the transformative power it holds.

The Science of Risk and Reward

Human evolution and psychology offer insights into our relationship with risk. Our ancestors faced constant threats and uncertainties, and those who took calculated risks often reaped significant rewards, such as new territories or vital resources. Today, while the nature of risks has evolved, the fundamental principle remains: taking risks is intrinsically linked to potential rewards.

Neurobiology of Risk-Taking:
The human brain's reward system, particularly the role of dopamine, highlights the exhilaration and fulfillment derived from risk-taking. When we successfully navigate risks, our brain releases dopamine, a neurotransmitter associated with pleasure and satisfaction, reinforcing the behavior.

Psychological Growth:
Psychological theories, such as those proposed by Abraham Maslow, suggest that stepping out of one's comfort zone is crucial for self-actualization. Experiencing and overcoming challenges is what propels individuals toward realizing their full potential.

Resilience and Adaptability:
Research in resilience psychology indicates that facing and overcoming risks strengthens adaptability, teaching us to navigate

future uncertainties with greater ease. Each risk taken is a lesson in resilience, enhancing our capacity to bounce back from setbacks.

The Personal Journey of Risk-Taking

Taking risks is as much about the external quest for achievement as it is about the internal journey of self-discovery and growth.

Discovering Your True Potential:
Only by pushing beyond the comfort zone can you discover the extent of your capabilities. Risk-taking challenges you to explore unknown facets of your character, talents, and determination.

Cultivating Courage and Confidence:
Each risk embarked upon builds a foundation of courage and self-confidence. The act of facing fears head-on transforms self-doubt into self-assurance, forging a stronger, more confident man in the process.

The Reward of Authentic Experiences:
The richest experiences often lie beyond the safety of the familiar. Taking risks opens the door to new adventures, relationships, and insights, enriching life with authentic, unforgettable moments.

Balancing Risk with Wisdom

While advocating for risk-taking, it's crucial to distinguish between reckless behavior and calculated risks. The art of successful risk-taking involves assessing potential outcomes, considering the consequences, and preparing as best as possible for the challenges ahead.

Informed Decision-Making:
Leveraging knowledge, insight, and foresight to make informed decisions about which risks are worth pursuing.

Risk Management:
Developing strategies to mitigate potential downsides, ensuring that even if things don't go as planned, the experience is still valuable for growth.

Embracing Failure as a Teacher:
Understanding that not all risks will lead to success, but every outcome is a learning opportunity that contributes to personal and professional development.

The Power of Risk-Taking

Embracing risk is a declaration of one's commitment to growth, adventure, and the pursuit of one's highest aspirations. It is a testament to the belief in oneself and the willingness to pursue what is meaningful, even in the face of uncertainty. For a man seeking to carve a path of significance, to leave a mark on the world, and to discover the depths of his own strength and capability, taking risks is not merely an option; it is a necessity.

Through the challenges and triumphs of risk-taking, you forge a life of richness and purpose, a life where each leap, each decision to step into the unknown, brings you closer to becoming the fullest expression of yourself. This is the essence of a life well-lived, marked not by the avoidance of risk, but by the courage to face it head-on.

The Importance of Saying No

In our journey through life, we often encounter crossroads where we must choose between saying yes to others' requests or standing firm and saying no. While the former might seem like the easiest path, laden with immediate gratification and approval, the latter, though seemingly arduous, leads to long-term benefits and personal growth. Saying no, contrary to popular belief, is not a sign of selfishness but a profound expression of self-respect and understanding of one's limits.

Why Saying No Is Necessary

Saying no is crucial for maintaining mental health and personal boundaries. When we constantly say yes to avoid disappointing others, we inadvertently set ourselves up for stress, burnout, and even resentment. Science supports this: studies in psychology emphasize the stress response triggered in our bodies when we overcommit. This stress can lead to chronic conditions such as hypertension and anxiety, significantly impacting our quality of life. Therefore, saying no is not just about rejecting a request; it's about protecting our well-being.

The Pitfall of Being a Pleaser

Being a pleaser might seem like a path to popularity and acceptance, but it's fraught with pitfalls. Pleasers often prioritize others' needs over their own, leading to a loss of self-identity and personal dissatisfaction. This behavior can stem from a fear of rejection or a deep-seated belief that one's worth is tied to how much they do for others. However, constantly seeking approval from others is a never-ending cycle that seldom leads to genuine self-fulfillment.

Embrace the Power of No

Saying no is empowering. It signifies a strong sense of self-awareness — knowing what you can handle and acknowledging your limits. This decision doesn't just benefit you; it also respects the person making the request by setting clear and honest boundaries. Remember, when you say no to things that don't align with your values or capabilities, you open up space and energy for opportunities that do.

The Science Behind Saying No
Neurologically, making decisions that align with our well-being, like saying no, activates parts of the brain associated with self-control and emotional regulation. This activation not only helps in immediate stress reduction but also strengthens these neural pathways, making it easier to make healthy decisions in the future. Furthermore, psychological research shows that individuals who assertively say no report higher levels of happiness and satisfaction, underscoring the profound impact of this simple act on our mental health.

A Personal Touch
I understand the fear and guilt that often accompany the act of saying no. It's a challenge I've faced many times. But with each no I've uttered, I've found a deeper sense of peace and self-respect. It's a journey of recognizing that your needs and well-being are paramount. Each time you say no, you're affirming your worth and taking a step toward a more balanced and fulfilling life.

In Conclusion
Saying no is an art and a critical life skill. It's about making choices that align with your well-being, values, and priorities. While it might not always be easy, the benefits are immense. It leads to better mental health, stronger relationships based on honesty and respect, and, ultimately, a life that truly feels like your own. So, the next time you're faced with a request that doesn't feel right, remember the power of saying no. It's not just a word; it's a pathway to a healthier, happier you.

The Importance of Money

In the tapestry of life, financial stability emerges as a crucial thread, weaving through aspects of personal freedom, security, and self-esteem. This chapter explores the significance of financial stability, not as an end in itself, but as a means to enrich one's life and relationships. It delves into how achieving financial stability can enhance personal well-being and, by extension, create a more fulfilling life.

The Psychological Impact of Financial Stability

Financial stability exerts a profound impact on our psychological well-being. A solid financial foundation can alleviate stress associated with financial insecurity, allowing for a more focused pursuit of personal goals and interests. Science supports this connection:

Reduced Stress and Anxiety:
Research in financial psychology has consistently shown that financial stability significantly reduces stress and anxiety levels. The assurance that comes with having financial resources contributes to a sense of safety and security.

Enhanced Self-Esteem:
Financial stability can boost self-esteem and self-worth. Being financially secure allows individuals to make choices that reflect their values and aspirations, fostering a sense of autonomy and self-respect.

Freedom to Pursue Personal Growth:
With financial stability, individuals have the freedom to invest in personal development, whether through education, travel, or pursuing hobbies. This freedom is instrumental in cultivating a well-rounded, fulfilling life.

Financial Stability and Social Relationships

While financial stability is an admirable goal for personal reasons, its role in attracting relationships, including romantic ones, should be approached with nuance. Attraction is multifaceted, encompassing emotional, intellectual, and physical dimensions. Financial stability can contribute to attractiveness by signaling the ability to provide and the presence of ambition and responsibility, traits often appreciated in a partner. However, the foundation of lasting relationships transcends material wealth, rooted in mutual respect, emotional connection, and shared values.

Confidence Attracts:
Confidence, often bolstered by financial stability, is a universally attractive trait. It reflects a sense of security in one's abilities and decisions, appealing to potential partners who value self-assuredness and reliability.

Shared Experiences:
Financial stability enables a variety of shared experiences, from travel to cultural events, enriching the relationship and creating lasting memories.

Security and Planning for the Future:
In the context of long-term relationships, financial stability provides a foundation for planning a future together, offering a sense of security and shared goals.

Achieving Financial Stability

Budgeting and Financial Planning:
Understanding and managing your finances through budgeting and planning are key steps toward financial stability. Tools and resources are available to help individuals learn these skills.

Investing in Your Future:
Consider investments and savings not just as financial strategies but as investments in your future well-being and freedom.

Continuous Learning and Growth:
Stay informed about financial management, and seek opportunities for personal and professional growth. Education and skill development can open doors to higher earning potential and financial security.

The True Value of Financial Stability

Financial stability is a valuable goal, contributing to personal well-being, confidence, and the ability to fully engage in life's opportunities. It supports personal growth, enriches relationships, and provides a foundation for pursuing one's passions and goals. However, it's important to remember that financial stability is most meaningful when it serves as a tool for creating a life that aligns with your values and aspirations, not as the sole measure of success or attractiveness.

In navigating the path to financial stability, the journey is as significant as the destination, offering lessons in discipline, planning, and resilience that extend far beyond the financial realm.

The Importance of Becoming Smarter

Intelligence, in its broadest sense, encompasses much more than academic prowess or mastery of a particular skill set. It's about cultivating a curious mind, a willingness to learn, and an ability to engage deeply with the world around you. This chapter delves into why intellectual growth is not only inherently valuable but also plays a significant role in forming meaningful relationships and attracting partners who value depth, conversation, and shared growth.

The Multifaceted Nature of Intelligence

Intelligence is diverse. It includes emotional intelligence (the ability to understand and manage emotions), social intelligence (the capacity to navigate social situations effectively), and cultural intelligence (the ability to relate and work effectively across cultures). Each of these dimensions contributes to a well-rounded, engaging individual who brings depth and understanding to their interactions.

Why Intellectual Growth Matters

Enhances Personal Fulfillment:
Engaging in lifelong learning and intellectual pursuits enriches your life, providing a sense of accomplishment and satisfaction. This intrinsic motivation to grow and learn is linked to higher levels of personal happiness and well-being.

Attracts Like-minded Individuals:
A commitment to intellectual growth often attracts like-minded individuals who value depth and substance in relationships. Shared intellectual interests can form the basis of deep, meaningful connections.

Improves Communication Skills:
Learning about diverse subjects and cultures enhances your ability to communicate effectively with a wide range of people. This adaptability and empathy make you more approachable and relatable, qualities that are attractive in any relationship.

Fosters Creativity and Problem-Solving:
Intellectual curiosity drives creativity and innovation. A smart individual is often a problem solver, able to approach challenges with fresh perspectives and solutions, which is a valuable trait in both personal and professional realms.

Strategies for Cultivating Intelligence

Embrace Lifelong Learning:
Adopt the mindset that learning doesn't end with formal education. Seek out books, online courses, lectures, and podcasts on a variety of topics that interest you.

Travel and Experience Different Cultures:
Traveling exposes you to new ideas, customs, and ways of thinking, significantly broadening your horizons and enhancing your cultural and social intelligence.

Engage in Thoughtful Conversations:
Seek out discussions with individuals who challenge you intellectually and offer different perspectives. These conversations can stimulate your thinking and broaden your understanding of complex issues.

Practice Critical Thinking:
Challenge yourself to think critically about the information you encounter. Ask questions, seek evidence, and consider multiple viewpoints to develop a well-rounded understanding of topics.

Cultivate Emotional Intelligence:
Pay attention to your emotions and those of others. Practice empathy, active listening, and effective communication to deepen your emotional insights and connections.

Intelligence as a Journey, Not a Destination

Becoming smarter is a journey of continuous exploration, curiosity, and growth. It's about enriching your life with knowledge and experiences that broaden your understanding of the world and yourself. This journey not only enhances personal fulfillment but also makes you a more engaging, empathetic, and attractive partner to those who value depth and intellectual connection.

Remember, the pursuit of intelligence is not about boasting or competing but about the joy of learning and the doors it opens in all areas of life, including personal relationships. By embracing the path of intellectual growth, you invest in your most valuable asset—yourself.

The Importance of Life Experience

Life, in all its complexity, offers a vast landscape of experiences that shape who we are, how we see the world, and how we connect with others. This chapter celebrates the myriad ways in which life experiences, from the mundane to the extraordinary, contribute to our personal growth and enhance our relationships. It delves into the science behind experiential learning, the value of diverse experiences, and how embracing life's journey can make us more well-rounded, empathetic, and engaging individuals.

The Value of Diverse Life Experiences

Life experiences, ranging from travel and adventure to overcoming challenges and engaging in different cultures, enrich our understanding of the world and ourselves. These experiences contribute significantly to our intellectual and emotional development, making us more attractive to others who value depth and authenticity.

Broadening Perspectives:
Engaging with a wide array of cultures, beliefs, and lifestyles broadens our perspectives, fostering a more inclusive and empathetic worldview. This openness and adaptability are highly valued in personal and professional relationships.

Enhancing Emotional Intelligence:
Experiences, especially those that challenge us, enhance our emotional intelligence. They teach us resilience, empathy, and the complexity of human emotions, allowing for deeper connections with others.

Cultivating Curiosity and Creativity:
Diverse experiences fuel our curiosity and creativity, driving innovation and problem-solving skills. A curious mind is always learning, exploring, and seeking to understand, traits that contribute to a vibrant and engaging personality.

The Science Behind Experiential Learning

Experiential learning, or learning through doing, has been shown to have a profound impact on cognitive and emotional development. The process of actively engaging with new experiences facilitates deeper learning and retention of information, enhancing our cognitive abilities and emotional resilience.

Neuroplasticity:
New experiences can stimulate neuroplasticity, the brain's ability to form new neural connections throughout life. This plasticity is crucial for learning, memory, and adaptation to new challenges.

Stress and Growth:
While excessive stress can be harmful, moderate stress experienced during challenging experiences can promote personal growth and resilience. The concept of "eustress," or positive stress, highlights how certain challenges can be beneficial for our development.

Happiness and Fulfillment:
Psychological research links diverse and rich experiences to higher levels of happiness and fulfillment. Experiences, rather than material possessions, provide lasting memories and a sense of satisfaction that contribute to our overall well-being.

Embracing Life Experiences

To fully embrace life's richness, it's essential to step out of your comfort zone and seek out new experiences. Whether it's learning a new language, traveling to an unfamiliar place, or taking up a new hobby, each new experience adds a thread to the tapestry of your life.

Be Open to New Opportunities:
Cultivate a mindset that welcomes new opportunities, even if they seem daunting at first. Each experience is a chance to learn and grow.

Seek Meaningful Connections:
Engage deeply with the people and cultures you encounter. Meaningful connections can provide insights and perspectives that enrich your understanding of the world.

Reflect on Your Experiences:
Take time to reflect on your experiences and the lessons they offer. Reflection is a key component of learning and personal growth.

The Journey of Experiential Enrichment

Life's journey is not just about the destinations reached but about the experiences gathered along the way. These experiences shape us, teach us, and connect us to the world in profound ways. By embracing the richness of life's experiences, we become more well-rounded, empathetic, and engaging individuals, capable of forming deep and meaningful connections with others.

In the pursuit of personal growth and fulfilling relationships, let the wealth of your experiences be your guide. Each new adventure, challenge, and encounter is an opportunity to expand your horizons and enrich your life in ways you never imagined.

The Importance of Staying Away From Porn

In today's digital age, the accessibility of pornography has made it a pervasive part of many lives. While it's a personal choice, growing evidence suggests that stepping away from pornography can have significant benefits for mental health, relationships, and personal growth. This chapter delves into the reasons to consider this path, supported by scientific research, and offers guidance on making this change in a way that's respectful to oneself and one's journey of personal development.

Understanding the Impact

The consumption of pornography has been linked to various psychological and relational challenges. While the experiences can vary widely among individuals, here are some researched effects:

Mental Health Concerns:
Studies indicate a correlation between heavy pornography use and increased symptoms of depression, anxiety, and stress. The mechanisms are complex and multifaceted, involving factors like unrealistic expectations, feelings of guilt or shame, and the potential for addictive behaviors.

Relationship Dynamics:
Research suggests that pornography can affect relationship satisfaction. It may create unrealistic expectations, reduce intimacy, and lead to conflicts or trust issues between partners.

Cognitive Function and Perception:
Prolonged exposure to pornography can influence one's perception of sexuality, relationships, and even self-worth. This altered perception can impact real-life interactions and expectations.

The Benefits of Quitting

Choosing to quit or reduce pornography consumption can lead to numerous benefits, enhancing personal well-being and the quality of one's relationships.

Improved Mental Health:
Many report feeling clearer, less burdened by guilt or shame, and more positive about themselves after reducing their consumption of pornography. This clarity can contribute to lower levels of depression and anxiety.

Enhanced Relationships:
Fostering intimacy and trust in relationships can be easier without the influence of pornography. This can lead to deeper connections, more satisfying sexual experiences, and improved communication with partners.

Increased Productivity and Focus:
Redirecting the time and energy spent on pornography towards productive activities or hobbies can lead to personal achievements, skill development, and a more fulfilling use of one's time.

Greater Self-Control:
Overcoming the habit of watching pornography can enhance one's sense of self-control and willpower, which can be applied to other areas of life, leading to a greater sense of personal agency.

Steps Towards Change

Making a change involves acknowledging the challenge, understanding the reasons behind the decision to quit, and taking concrete steps towards a new habit or lifestyle.

Acknowledge and Reflect:
Begin by acknowledging the desire to change and reflecting on the reasons and motivations behind this decision. Understanding your 'why' is crucial for sustained change.

Seek Support:
Whether it's through friends, family, or professionals like therapists, support is vital. There are also online forums and groups dedicated to helping individuals through this process.

Develop New Habits:
Fill the time previously spent on pornography with new, enriching activities. Whether it's exercise, learning a new skill, or engaging in creative pursuits, find something that adds value to your life.

Practice Self-Compassion:
Change is a process that often involves setbacks. Practice self-compassion and patience with yourself as you navigate this journey.

A Path of Personal Empowerment

Choosing to step away from pornography is a deeply personal decision, one that can lead to significant personal growth, improved mental health, and richer, more fulfilling relationships. It's about reclaiming your time, energy, and focus, directing them towards the aspects of life that bring true joy, satisfaction, and connection.

This journey is not just about quitting a habit; it's about embracing a lifestyle that aligns with your values, goals, and the person you aspire to be. It's a path of empowerment, clarity, and personal freedom.

The Importance of Adaptability

In a world that's constantly evolving, the ability to adapt is more than a skill—it's a necessity. For a man navigating the complexities of modern life, adaptability is not just about surviving; it's about thriving. This chapter explores the critical importance of adaptability, blending motivational insights with scientific evidence to illustrate how this trait can transform challenges into opportunities for growth and success.

Understanding Adaptability

Adaptability refers to the capacity to adjust one's thoughts, behaviors, and actions in response to new information, changing conditions, or unexpected obstacles. It's about being flexible in the face of life's uncertainties and finding creative solutions to problems. For men, embodying adaptability means navigating life's changes with resilience, foresight, and an open mind.

The Science Behind Adaptability

Research in psychology and neuroscience highlights adaptability as a key determinant of success and well-being. Studies show that individuals who exhibit high levels of adaptability are better equipped to manage stress, overcome adversity, and achieve their goals. This flexibility is linked to a growth mindset, where challenges are seen as opportunities to learn and evolve rather than insurmountable barriers.

1. Resilience in the Face of Adversity
Adaptability fosters resilience, enabling men to bounce back from setbacks with greater strength and wisdom. Whether it's a personal loss, a career change, or a failed venture, the capacity to adapt ensures that each experience contributes to personal growth rather than defeat.

2. Navigating Career and Life Transitions
In today's fast-paced world, career paths are no longer linear. Technological advancements, economic shifts, and global trends demand a workforce that's flexible and ready to learn. Adaptability empowers men to seize new opportunities, pivot in their careers, and stay relevant in an ever-changing job market.

3. Enhancing Relationships
Adaptability is crucial in building and maintaining healthy relationships. It involves compromising, understanding different perspectives, and adjusting to the evolving dynamics of personal and professional relationships. This flexibility fosters deeper connections and mutual respect.

4. Promoting Personal Growth
Embracing adaptability encourages lifelong learning and self-discovery. It motivates men to explore new interests, develop new skills, and step out of their comfort zones. This journey of continuous improvement enriches life with diverse experiences and insights.

Cultivating Adaptability

Developing adaptability requires intention and practice. Here are strategies to enhance this essential trait:

Cultivate a Growth Mindset:
Embrace challenges as opportunities for growth. View failures as lessons rather than defeats.

Stay Curious:
Foster a sense of curiosity about the world. Seek out new experiences and knowledge.

Practice Flexibility:
In decision-making and problem-solving, consider multiple paths and be open to changing course as needed.

Build Emotional Intelligence:
Develop the ability to manage your emotions and understand those of others, enhancing your capacity to navigate changes in relationships and environments.

Reflect and Learn:
Regularly reflect on your experiences. Identify what you've learned and how you can apply those lessons in the future.

Conclusion

Adaptability is the cornerstone of a fulfilling and successful life. It equips men with the resilience to face life's uncertainties, the agility to pursue new opportunities, and the openness to grow from every experience. In embracing adaptability, you unlock your full potential, ready to navigate the ever-changing landscape of life with confidence, creativity, and an unwavering spirit of adventure.

Remember, the journey of life is not about the destination but about how you adapt and grow along the way. Embrace change, stay flexible, and watch as the world opens up with endless possibilities.

The Importance of Patience

In the fast-paced rhythm of modern life, patience is a virtue often overlooked, yet it remains one of the most powerful traits a man can cultivate. This chapter delves into the essence of patience, not just as the ability to wait, but as a profound strength that enables individuals to navigate life's challenges with grace, resilience, and foresight. Through motivational insights and scientific evidence, we explore how patience impacts personal growth, relationships, and overall well-being, offering practical advice on nurturing this transformative quality.

Understanding Patience

Patience is more than enduring delay or tolerating provocation; it's an active engagement with time, emotions, and circumstances. It's the art of being present, the strength to remain calm, and the wisdom to act with intention rather than impulse. For men striving to lead lives of significance and fulfillment, patience offers a path to deeper understanding and more meaningful achievements.

The Science Behind Patience

Research in psychology and neuroscience highlights the benefits of patience, linking it to better mental health, higher life satisfaction, and stronger interpersonal relationships. Patience is associated with decreased levels of stress and anxiety, as it involves a more thoughtful approach to problem-solving and decision-making, reducing the impulsivity that often leads to regret.

Enhanced Emotional Regulation:
Studies show that patient individuals exhibit better control over their emotions, leading to more positive interactions and less conflict in relationships.

Improved Decision Making:
The ability to wait and consider all options leads to more informed and effective decisions. Patience allows for the gathering of additional information and a deeper evaluation of potential outcomes.

Greater Achievement:
Patience is key to achieving long-term goals. Research suggests that those who exhibit patience are more likely to persevere in the face of challenges, leading to greater success in personal and professional endeavors.

Cultivating Patience in a Fast-Paced World

Developing patience in today's instant-gratification society can be challenging, but it is immensely rewarding. Here are strategies to nurture patience:

Practice Mindfulness:
Engage in mindfulness exercises to enhance your awareness of the present moment. This practice helps in recognizing and managing impulsive reactions, fostering a more patient mindset.

Set Realistic Expectations:
Adjusting your expectations to reflect reality can significantly reduce frustration and impatience. Understand that some things take time and that perseverance is often required to achieve worthwhile outcomes.

Develop Empathy:
Trying to understand situations from others' perspectives can cultivate patience. Empathy encourages a more compassionate response to the actions and needs of others, reducing feelings of irritation and urgency.

Embrace Delay as Opportunity:
View waiting times as opportunities for growth or relaxation. Whether it's practicing deep breathing during a traffic jam or using extra time to learn something new, transforming delays into productive moments can lessen the weight of impatience.

Reflect on Past Successes:
Remembering times when patience led to positive outcomes can reinforce the value of this virtue. Reflect on how patience has previously served you well, using these instances as motivation to persist.

The Reward of Patience

The rewards of patience extend far beyond immediate gains. It enriches life with a sense of calm, deepens relationships through understanding and respect, and fosters a resilient spirit capable of overcoming any challenge. Patience is the foundation upon which lasting success and fulfillment are built.

Conclusion

Patience is a testament to a man's strength, a quiet declaration of confidence in one's abilities and faith in the unfolding of time. It's a challenge, certainly, in an age that prizes speed and efficiency, but its rewards are timeless. By cultivating patience, you stand as a beacon of calm in the tumult of the world, ready to seize the right opportunities and navigate life's storms with unwavering resolve.

Remember, the greatest achievements often come to those who wait, not passively, but with an active and hopeful patience that transforms dreams into reality.

The Art of Decision Making

Decision making is an art, a skill that weaves together the threads of thoughtfulness and speed to create a tapestry of successful outcomes. In the fast-paced world we live in, the ability to make quick and rational decisions is not just a virtue but a necessity. It's about striking a balance between deliberation and action, ensuring that our choices lead us to our desired destinations.

The Importance of Quick and Rational Decisions
Making decisions quickly and rationally is crucial in a world where opportunities come and go in the blink of an eye. Quick decision-making allows us to seize these fleeting chances, propelling us forward toward our goals. On the other hand, rationality ensures that our choices are grounded in logic, reason, and a clear understanding of our objectives and the potential consequences of our actions.

But why is this blend of speed and rationality so important? Science provides an answer. Neurological studies show that our brains are wired to make decisions based on a mix of emotional and rational inputs. When we make decisions quickly, we often rely on what's known as the "gut feeling," which is our brain's way of using past experiences and emotional knowledge to guide us. Rational thinking, however, involves the more analytical parts of our brain, ensuring that our decisions are well-considered and not just impulsive reactions.

The Science Behind Decision Making
The prefrontal cortex plays a crucial role in our decision-making processes. It's responsible for weighing the pros and cons, predicting outcomes, and integrating emotional signals. When we make decisions, a part of the brain called the ventromedial prefrontal cortex evaluates the emotional value of the choices, while the dorsolateral prefrontal cortex is involved in rational thinking and controlling

impulsive behavior. Balancing these aspects leads to decisions that are both quick and rational.

Moreover, psychological research has shown that decision-making skills can be significantly improved with practice. By consciously working on making our decision-making process more efficient, we can train our brains to find that sweet spot between speed and rationality more quickly.

Embracing the Art
The art of decision-making is about embracing the power within us to shape our lives. It's recognizing that while not every decision will be perfect, the act of making a decision is a declaration of our agency. It's about understanding that our mistakes are not failures but lessons that guide our future choices.

Incorporating both quickness and rationality in our decisions doesn't mean acting hastily or overanalyzing every choice. It means listening to our intuition while also considering the facts at hand. It's about asking ourselves the right questions, evaluating our options, and then confidently taking a step in the direction we choose.

Conclusion

The art of decision-making is a skill that can be honed over time, with each choice we make. By learning to trust ourselves and by applying a blend of quick thinking and rational analysis, we can navigate the complexities of life with grace and confidence. Remember, the journey of a thousand miles begins with a single step — a decision. Let's make our decisions our stepping stones to success.

The Art of Storytelling

Storytelling is a profound and ancient art form that has woven the fabric of human culture and society through ages. It's an art that transcends mere entertainment, serving as a bridge connecting individuals, communities, and generations. At the heart of storytelling lies the power to evoke emotions, impart wisdom, and inspire change. But storytelling isn't just for authors, filmmakers, or public speakers—it's an essential skill for everyone, influencing various aspects of our personal and professional lives.

The Science of Storytelling
The significance of storytelling is deeply rooted in science. Neurologically, stories have a unique way of engaging our brains. When we hear a story, not only are the language processing parts of our brain activated, but all other areas of the brain that we would use when experiencing the events of the story are too. This means that stories allow us to feel emotions, visualize scenes, and understand complex information in a more profound way than facts and figures alone can provide.

Research has shown that when we listen to stories, our levels of oxytocin increase. Oxytocin is a hormone that plays a role in empathy and relationship-building. This suggests that storytelling can build connections between people, fostering a sense of trust and cooperation. Furthermore, a compelling narrative can significantly affect our attitudes, beliefs, and decisions by embedding memories, ideas, and values.

Quick and Rational Decisions in Storytelling
The art of storytelling also encompasses the importance of making quick and rational decisions. Whether you're crafting a narrative, deciding the direction of your story, or choosing the right moment to deliver a crucial piece of information, these decisions shape how effectively your story resonates with the audience. Quick decisions can

capture spontaneous moments that add authenticity and relatability to your tale. Simultaneously, rational decisions ensure that your story remains coherent, engaging, and impactful, maintaining the integrity of its message and purpose.

Cultivating Your Storytelling Skills

Listen and Observe:
Great stories often come from being a keen observer of life. Listen to others, observe the world around you, and draw inspiration from everyday moments.

Embrace Vulnerability:
Don't shy away from sharing your failures and fears. It's through vulnerability that stories become relatable and powerful.

Understand Your Audience:
Tailor your story to resonate with your listeners. Consider their interests, experiences, and emotions to make your narrative more impactful.

Practice Makes Perfect:
Like any art, storytelling improves with practice. Share your stories often, seek feedback, and refine your craft.

Study Master Storytellers:
Learn from the best. Read widely, watch compelling movies, and listen to engaging podcasts. Analyze how these storytellers craft their narratives, build tension, and develop characters.

Create Multi-Dimensional Characters: Develop characters with depth and complexity. Give them desires, fears, strengths, and weaknesses. This makes them relatable and memorable to your audience.

Incorporate Sensory Details:
Use descriptive language to engage the five senses. Describe what characters see, hear, smell, taste, and touch to immerse your audience fully in the story.

Use Metaphors and Similes:
These literary devices enrich your narrative by drawing comparisons that illuminate concepts in vivid and imaginative ways.

Build a Strong Setting:
The environment where your story takes place can significantly impact its mood and tone. Craft your settings with as much care as you do your characters.

Manage Pace Wisely:
Vary the pace of your story according to its needs. Use shorter sentences and scenes to build tension or action, and longer ones for reflection or detail.

Incorporate Conflict and Resolution:
Every compelling story has a conflict that needs resolving. This drives the narrative forward and keeps your audience engaged.

Show, Don't Just Tell:
Instead of simply telling your audience what happens, show them through action, dialogue, and thought processes. This makes the story more engaging and believable.

Storytelling is an essential skill for men, offering a multitude of benefits that extend beyond the mere ability to entertain. It's a tool that can significantly enhance personal, social, and professional aspects of life. Here's why a man needs to be good at storytelling:

1. Enhances Communication Skills
Storytelling elevates communication by adding depth and emotion to the information being shared. It transforms simple messages into engaging narratives, making them more memorable and impactful. This skill is invaluable in both personal relationships and professional environments, where clear and compelling communication is often the key to success.

2. Builds Stronger Connections
Stories have the power to bridge gaps and bring people closer. By sharing personal stories, men can foster deeper connections with friends, family, and partners. Storytelling reveals vulnerabilities and strengths, allowing listeners to empathize and understand the storyteller on a more profound level.

3. Improves Persuasion and Influence
In the world of business and leadership, storytelling is a critical tool for persuasion and influence. A well-told story can inspire teams, sell products, and convey visions in a way that facts and data alone cannot. It helps in framing challenges, solutions, and successes in a relatable context, making the persuasive process more effective.

4. Facilitates Learning and Teaching
Good storytellers are also effective educators. Stories can simplify complex concepts, making them easier to understand and remember. Whether it's teaching a child, mentoring a colleague, or sharing knowledge with peers, storytelling can enhance the learning experience and ensure the message sticks.

5. Encourages Empathy and Understanding
Storytelling fosters empathy by allowing the listener to walk in someone else's shoes, even if just for a moment. For men, this can be an invaluable way to understand different perspectives, cultures, and experiences, broadening their worldview and enhancing their emotional intelligence.

6. Boosts Creativity and Problem-Solving

Creating and telling stories requires imagination and creativity. It's a practice that challenges men to think outside the box, explore different outcomes, and view situations from various angles. This not only makes storytelling an enriching creative outlet but also sharpens problem-solving skills.

7. Leaves a Legacy

Stories are one of the most powerful ways to leave a legacy. They can pass on wisdom, values, and experiences to future generations. For many men, storytelling is a way to ensure their lessons and life experiences are remembered and cherished.

8. Enhances Self-Understanding

The process of crafting stories often requires reflection on personal experiences, decisions, and growth. For men, this introspection can lead to greater self-awareness and a better understanding of their own journey through life.

9. Navigates Social Settings with Ease

Being a good storyteller can make social interactions more engaging and enjoyable. Whether it's breaking the ice in a new group, entertaining guests at a dinner party, or captivating an audience at a social event, storytelling skills can make a man more charismatic and socially adept.

Conclusion

The art of storytelling is a timeless skill that holds the power to enlighten, entertain, and inspire. It bridges gaps, builds connections, and shapes our understanding of the world and ourselves. By harnessing the science and emotion behind storytelling, we can all become architects of narratives that not only capture attention but also touch hearts and change minds. Remember, each of us has a story worth telling; it's up to us to share it with the world.

The Art of Being Independent

In the journey of life, the art of being independent stands as a majestic tower, visible from miles around, guiding us towards self-reliance, resilience, and freedom. It's not just about physical or financial independence but encompasses emotional, psychological, and intellectual realms as well. Being independent means not tethering your well-being, happiness, or decision-making process entirely to external factors—be it people, medicine, supplements, or societal expectations.

Why Independence Matters
Independence is a cornerstone of a fulfilling life. It empowers you to make choices that align with your values, navigate challenges with your inner compass, and live authentically. Dependence, especially when excessive, can lead to a loss of self, where decisions are no longer your own but are instead heavily influenced or dictated by external factors.

Science backs the importance of independence for mental health and well-being. Studies in psychology emphasize that autonomy—a core component of independence—is linked to higher satisfaction in life, better mental health, and improved resilience. When you are independent, you are more likely to engage in activities that are meaningful to you, leading to a deeper sense of fulfillment.

The Dangers of Overdependence
Relying too much on others for emotional support or decision-making can hinder personal growth. While interdependence (mutual reliance) is healthy, overdependence can stifle your ability to solve problems, reduce your self-confidence, and even lead to feelings of helplessness. Similarly, overreliance on medicine, supplements, or other external aids for health and well-being can sometimes prevent individuals from pursuing holistic lifestyle changes that address the root causes of their issues.

Cultivating Independence

Embrace Self-Discovery:
Spend time alone, reflect on your values, passions, and goals. Self-discovery is the foundation of independence; it helps you understand who you are beyond societal labels and expectations.

Develop Critical Thinking:
Learn to question, analyze, and evaluate information. Critical thinking fosters intellectual independence, enabling you to form your opinions and beliefs based on evidence rather than blindly following others.

Strengthen Emotional Resilience:
Emotional independence involves managing your feelings and reactions without undue reliance on others. Techniques such as mindfulness, meditation, and cognitive-behavioral strategies can enhance your emotional regulation skills.

Practice Decision-Making:
Make small decisions on your own and gradually tackle more significant choices. Each decision strengthens your confidence and reinforces your ability to stand by your convictions.

Cultivate Financial Literacy:
Understanding and managing your finances is a practical aspect of independence. Educate yourself on budgeting, saving, investing, and financial planning to take control of your economic future.

Prioritize Health and Wellness:
While medicine and supplements have their place, fostering a lifestyle that includes a balanced diet, regular exercise, and sufficient rest is crucial. This holistic approach reduces overdependence on external aids for health.

Seek Knowledge and Skills:
Lifelong learning and skill acquisition enhance your ability to be self-sufficient. Whether it's fixing a leaky faucet or learning to cook healthy meals, each new skill adds a layer to your independence.

Conclusion

The art of being independent is a continuous process of learning, growing, and adapting. It's about building a life where you are the author of your story, guided by your inner voice. Independence doesn't mean isolating yourself or rejecting help; it's about having the strength to stand alone when necessary and the wisdom to seek support when needed.

The Art of Negotiation

Negotiation is not just a skill for boardrooms and business deals; it's an essential part of everyday life. Whether you're discussing salary, resolving conflicts, or planning a trip with friends, the principles of negotiation come into play. This chapter delves into the art of negotiation, offering insights into how to approach negotiations not as battles to be won, but as opportunities for mutual gain. With a focus on motivational guidance and grounded in scientific research, we explore how to refine this skill to enhance both personal and professional aspects of your life.

Understanding Negotiation

At its core, negotiation is the process of trying to reach an agreement that is mutually beneficial to all parties involved. It requires a blend of communication, psychology, and strategy. The art lies in balancing assertiveness with empathy, understanding with persuasion, and compromise with ambition.

1. Preparation is Key
Before entering any negotiation, preparation is crucial. This involves understanding your goals, the limits of what you're willing to accept, and what you can offer. Research suggests that negotiators who enter discussions with clear objectives and background knowledge are more likely to achieve outcomes that align with their interests.

2. Listening Actively
Effective negotiation is rooted in active listening. By genuinely paying attention to the other party's needs and concerns, you can identify common ground and areas for compromise. Studies in communication have shown that active listening not only facilitates better outcomes but also fosters a positive rapport between parties.

3. Emphasize Win-Win Solutions

Approaching negotiations with a win-win mindset, where both parties feel they have gained from the agreement, is essential for long-term success. This approach builds trust and lays the groundwork for future cooperation. Psychological research supports that negotiations approached with cooperative strategies result in more mutually beneficial outcomes than those approached with competitive tactics.

4. Communicate Clearly and Confidently

Clear and confident communication conveys your positions and interests effectively. Assertiveness, combined with respect for the other party, ensures that your voice is heard without alienating or offending. Behavioral studies have found that assertive communication is linked to higher satisfaction levels in negotiation outcomes.

5. Be Willing to Adapt

Flexibility is a valuable asset in negotiations. Being open to alternative solutions and willing to adjust your strategy based on new information can lead to better, more creative outcomes. This adaptability signals to the other party that you are committed to finding a mutually satisfactory solution.

6. Know When to Walk Away

Understanding your bottom line and being prepared to walk away if terms cannot be met protects you from agreeing to unfavorable conditions. This principle, grounded in the concept of BATNA (Best Alternative to a Negotiated Agreement), is crucial for maintaining your interests.

7. Practice Empathy and Respect

Empathy allows you to see the negotiation from the other party's perspective, helping to identify what they value and why. Treating the other party with respect, regardless of the negotiation's outcome, maintains relationships and opens the door for future interactions.

Conclusion

Mastering the art of negotiation is a journey that extends beyond learning tactics and strategies; it's about developing a mindset that values mutual respect, understanding, and the pursuit of shared goals. By honing your negotiation skills, you equip yourself with the tools to navigate life's challenges and opportunities with confidence, turning everyday conversations into chances for growth and connection.

Remember, every negotiation is a step toward refining your ability to communicate, persuade, and collaborate effectively. Embrace each opportunity with an open mind, a prepared strategy, and a commitment to fairness, and watch as doors open to possibilities previously unimagined.

Cultivating Leadership Skills

Leadership is an art, a journey of continuous growth and self-discovery. It's about inspiring others, making impactful decisions, and leading by example. Cultivating leadership skills is not just for the CEOs and managers of the world; it's a valuable pursuit for anyone, at any stage in life. Whether you're leading a project team, managing a household, or simply guiding your own life path, leadership skills can illuminate the way.

The Essence of Leadership
At its core, leadership is about influence. It's how you affect the people around you, the environment you operate in, and how you navigate the challenges that come your way. But what makes a good leader? Is it the ability to make tough decisions, the capacity to inspire, or perhaps the integrity to stand by one's values? In truth, it's all of these and more.

The Science Behind Leadership
Research in psychology and neuroscience has shed light on the qualities that distinguish effective leaders. Emotional intelligence, for instance, plays a pivotal role. This encompasses self-awareness, empathy, and social skills – all crucial for understanding and motivating people. Studies have shown that leaders with high emotional intelligence can foster stronger team bonds, drive engagement, and navigate conflicts more effectively.

Another key aspect is decision-making. Leaders are often faced with complex choices under uncertainty. The science of decision-making has revealed that a blend of intuition and analytical thinking leads to better outcomes. Leaders benefit from being able to quickly assess a situation and use their knowledge and past experience to make informed choices.

Cognitive flexibility, the mental ability to switch between thinking about two different concepts, or to think about multiple concepts simultaneously, is also vital. It allows leaders to adapt to new information, shift strategies when necessary, and view challenges from various perspectives.

Cultivating Your Leadership Skills

Continuous Learning:
Leadership is a journey, not a destination. Stay curious, seek feedback, and always look for opportunities to grow.

Develop Emotional Intelligence:
Practice self-reflection, engage in active listening, and strive to understand the perspectives of others.

Balance Intuition with Analysis:
Trust your gut, but also gather information and weigh your options carefully before making decisions.

Foster Adaptability:
Stay open to new ideas and be willing to pivot when necessary. The best leaders are those who can navigate change with grace.

Lead with Integrity:
Your values are your compass. Be honest, transparent, and consistent in your actions and decisions.

Inspire and Empower:
Leadership is not about wielding power, but empowering others. Encourage initiative, celebrate achievements, and support your team in their growth.

Adding to the insightful exploration of leadership, here are some effective tips to further enhance your journey toward becoming a great leader:

Communicate Effectively:
Clear and concise communication is crucial. Be straightforward about your vision, goals, and expectations. Listen actively to your team's ideas and concerns, creating an environment where everyone feels heard and valued.

Practice Resilience:
Challenges and setbacks are inevitable. Demonstrate resilience by maintaining a positive attitude in the face of adversity. Show your team that obstacles are opportunities for growth and learning.

Foster a Culture of Trust:
Build trust within your team by being reliable, consistent, and fair. Trust fosters a positive working environment and encourages team members to take risks and innovate.

Encourage Diversity of Thought:
Welcome and value different perspectives and ideas. A diverse team brings a wealth of experiences and insights, leading to more creative and effective solutions.

Set Clear Goals and Expectations:
Provide your team with clear, achievable goals. This helps to align efforts, motivate team members, and measure progress effectively.

Be Decisive:
While it's important to gather information and consider different viewpoints, avoid paralysis by analysis. A good leader makes timely decisions and stands by them, ready to adjust as needed.

Show Appreciation and Recognition:
Acknowledge and reward your team's hard work and achievements. Recognition boosts morale and motivates team members to continue delivering their best.

Cultivate a Learning Environment:
Encourage continuous learning and development. Provide opportunities for your team to acquire new skills and knowledge, which can lead to innovation and improvement.

Be a Role Model:
Lead by example. Demonstrate the work ethic, integrity, and passion you wish to see in your team. Your behavior sets the standard for the team's culture and performance.

Promote Work-Life Balance:
Recognize the importance of balance in your team's lives. Encourage them to take time for themselves, which can lead to improved productivity and job satisfaction.

Embrace Feedback:
Seek and welcome feedback about your leadership style from peers, mentors, and team members. Use it as a tool for self-improvement and adaptation.

Practice Humility:
Be willing to admit mistakes and learn from them. Humility shows your team that it's okay to be imperfect and that every experience is a learning opportunity.

Each of these tips contributes to a comprehensive approach to leadership that values empathy, integrity, and continuous growth. By integrating these practices into your leadership journey, you're not just leading; you're transforming lives and making a lasting impact.

Leadership is a journey that constantly evolves, shaped by the lessons learned and the lives touched along the way. Embrace the journey with an open heart and mind, and watch as you and your team soar to new heights.

In Conclusion

Leadership is not reserved for a select few; it's a skill that can be cultivated by anyone with the determination to grow. It's about making a positive impact, whether in the lives of a few or many. By developing your leadership skills, you equip yourself with the tools to navigate life's challenges, inspire those around you, and leave a lasting legacy. Remember, every journey begins with a single step. Take that step today, and embark on your path to becoming a leader.

Developing Critical Thinking Skills

Critical Thinking is the art of analyzing and evaluating an issue or a situation with depth and open-mindedness to determine the best course of action. Critical thinking is not just a skill; it's a shield against misinformation, a catalyst for innovation, and a compass that guides us through the fog of biases and assumptions.

The Importance of Critical Thinking

Critical thinking compels us to look beyond the obvious, question the status quo, and challenge our preconceptions. It's about being curious, asking questions, and not taking information at face value. In a world teeming with information and myriad perspectives, the ability to sift through the noise, identify reliable sources, and arrive at well-informed conclusions is more important than ever.

Making quick and rational decisions is a cornerstone of critical thinking. The pace of modern life often requires us to make decisions swiftly. However, speed should not come at the expense of rationality. Critical thinking equips us with the tools to balance the need for prompt decisions with the necessity of ensuring they are well-reasoned and based on a thorough analysis of available information.

The Science Behind Critical Thinking

Neuroscience and psychology provide insights into how developing critical thinking skills can reshape our thinking processes. Engaging in critical thinking activities stimulates neural pathways associated with problem-solving and analytical thinking. This neural activation not only enhances our ability to process information efficiently but also improves our memory and learning capabilities.

Research in cognitive psychology highlights the role of critical thinking in overcoming cognitive biases and errors in judgment. By fostering an awareness of these biases and encouraging a more analytical approach to information, critical thinking helps us make more objective and accurate assessments.

Cultivating Your Critical Thinking Skills

Question Everything:
Adopt a questioning mindset. Ask who, what, where, when, why, and how. Don't accept information at face value; dig deeper.

Seek Diverse Perspectives:
Expose yourself to different viewpoints. This broadens your understanding and challenges your assumptions.

Analyze Arguments:
Evaluate the strength of arguments by considering the evidence supporting them and identifying any logical fallacies.

Reflect on Your Thinking Process:
Regularly reflect on your decision-making process. Identify any biases that may have influenced your conclusions.

Practice Problem-Solving:
Engage in activities that require problem-solving. Puzzles, strategy games, and brain teasers are excellent for this.

Read Widely and Critically:
Reading exposes you to new ideas and ways of thinking. Critically evaluate the arguments presented and consider their implications.

Conclusion

Developing critical thinking skills is a journey that requires dedication, curiosity, and an open mind. It's about becoming an active learner rather than a passive recipient of information. Remember, the goal of critical thinking is not to think more but to think better.

Building Emotional Resilience

In the vibrant tapestry of human experience, emotional resilience is the golden thread that strengthens our ability to navigate life's inevitable ups and downs. It's the inner fortitude that allows us to face challenges head-on, adapt to adversity, and emerge not just unscathed but stronger. Emotional resilience isn't about avoiding emotions or hardships but embracing them as opportunities for growth and learning.

The Importance of Emotional Resilience
Emotional resilience is crucial because it equips us with the psychological tools to handle stress, overcome obstacles, and bounce back from failures. In a world where change is the only constant, the ability to adapt and recover is invaluable. Resilient individuals can take life's setbacks in stride, viewing them not as insurmountable barriers but as challenges to be overcome. This mindset doesn't just help us cope with difficulties; it enables us to thrive amidst them.

Quick and Rational Decisions
Making quick and rational decisions is an essential aspect of building emotional resilience. In moments of crisis or stress, the ability to assess a situation swiftly and make informed choices can be the difference between faltering and flourishing. Quick decision-making allows us to respond effectively to immediate challenges, while rationality ensures that our actions are guided by logic, not just emotion. This balance is key to navigating life's storms with composure and confidence.

The Science Behind Emotional Resilience
From a scientific perspective, emotional resilience is fascinating. Neuroscience reveals that resilient individuals have more active prefrontal cortices—the area of the brain involved in planning complex cognitive behavior, personality expression, decision-making, and

moderating social behavior. This activity helps them think clearly and remain calm under pressure.

Psychological research also underscores the role of a positive outlook in building resilience. Optimism has been linked to better stress management and lower rates of depression. Resilient people tend to view problems as temporary and surmountable, which fuels their perseverance and drive to overcome adversity.

Moreover, studies in the field of psychoneuroimmunology (PNI) have shown that stress can weaken the immune system, making us more susceptible to illness. Emotional resilience, by helping us manage stress more effectively, can thus protect our physical health as well as our mental well-being.

Cultivating Your Emotional Resilience

Embrace Change:
View change as an inevitable and enriching part of life. Flexibility is at the heart of resilience.

Cultivate Optimism:
Focus on solutions rather than problems. Believe in your ability to find a way forward.

Develop a Support Network:
Surround yourself with people who uplift and support you. Relationships are crucial for resilience.

Practice Self-Compassion:
Be kind to yourself. Recognize that setbacks are part of being human and allow yourself to learn from them.

Take Care of Your Physical Health:
Exercise regularly, eat well, and get enough sleep. A healthy body supports a resilient mind.

Learn Stress Management Techniques:
Incorporate practices such as mindfulness, meditation, or deep breathing into your daily routine to help manage stress.

Conclusion

Building emotional resilience is a profound and personal journey. It's about discovering your inner strength, learning from life's challenges, and emerging stronger and more adaptable. Remember, resilience isn't a trait you're born with; it's a skill you can develop. With each step you take, with each challenge you overcome, you're not just surviving; you're thriving.

Developing a Positive Mindset

Cultivating a positive mindset is akin to setting sail towards a horizon of endless possibilities. It's about steering the ship of your life away from the stormy seas of negativity and towards the calm, radiant waters of positivity. This voyage is not just about enjoying the sunshine; it's about becoming a beacon of light for yourself and those around you.

The Perils of Negativity
The world can sometimes feel like a torrent of negativity, with challenges and setbacks lurking around every corner. Science tells us that our brains have a built-in negativity bias, a survival mechanism hardwired from our days in the wild, constantly on the lookout for threats. While this bias helped our ancestors survive, in today's world, it often leads us to overemphasize negative experiences, overshadowing the positive ones.

Negativity can drain your energy, cloud your judgment, and hinder your growth. It's a weight that pulls you down, making each step forward feel like a battle. But here's the empowering truth: you have the power to cut this weight loose, to choose not to dwell in the shadows of negativity but to bask in the light of positivity.

The Pleaser's Dilemma
Trying to please everyone is a trap. It's an exhausting, never-ending cycle that leaves little room for your own happiness and growth. The desire to be liked by everyone can lead you to compromise your values, silence your voice, and lose sight of who you are. Remember, your worth is not measured by how much you conform to others' expectations but by how authentically you live your life.

Science supports the idea that trying to please everyone is detrimental to our well-being. Studies in psychology show that people-pleasers often experience higher levels of stress and lower levels of self-esteem. Breaking free from the need to please is not about becoming indifferent to others but about finding a healthy balance where you can be kind and assertive, caring for others while also caring for yourself.

Cultivating Positivity:
Cultivating a positive mindset is not just wishful thinking; it's a practice supported by science. Neuroplasticity, the brain's ability to form new neural connections throughout life, means that with consistent practice, you can train your brain to lean more towards positivity. Engaging in positive thinking activates areas of the brain associated with emotional control, stress reduction, and happiness.

Furthermore, research in the field of positive psychology has shown that individuals with a positive outlook have better cardiovascular health, are more resilient to stress, and tend to live longer, happier lives. Positivity has been linked to improved creativity, problem-solving abilities, and overall mental and physical health.

Strategies for Developing a Positive Mindset

Limit Exposure to Negativity:
Be mindful of the media you consume, the conversations you engage in, and the thoughts you entertain. Surround yourself with positivity.

Practice Gratitude:
Start and end your day by reflecting on things you're thankful for. Gratitude shifts your focus from what's lacking to what's abundant.

Cultivate Self-Compassion:
Treat yourself with kindness and understanding. Speak to yourself as you would to a dear friend.

Set Healthy Boundaries:
Learn to say no. Protecting your time and energy is essential for maintaining positivity.

Engage in Positive Affirmations:
Start your day with affirmations that reinforce your worth, strength, and ability to face challenges.

Foster Optimism:
Look for the silver lining in every situation. Believe in the possibility of good outcomes.

Connect with Positive People:
Surround yourself with individuals who uplift and inspire you. Positivity is contagious.

Embrace Personal Growth:
View challenges as opportunities to learn and grow. Every setback is a step forward in disguise.

In conclusion, developing a positive mindset is a journey of a thousand miles that begins with a single step—a step taken with intention, courage, and an open heart. It's about choosing to see the beauty in life, believing in the goodness within and around you, and walking the path of positivity with conviction and grace. Remember, the light at the end of the tunnel is not an illusion; the tunnel is.

Developing Persistence

In the grand adventure of life, persistence is the compass that guides us through storms, over mountains, and across deserts to reach our destination. It's the relentless voice that whispers, "Try once more," when the world shouts, "Give up." Developing persistence is not just about stubbornly pushing forward; it's about cultivating a mindset that sees beyond temporary setbacks to the broader horizon of possibilities.

The Power of Persistence
Persistence is the silent engine that drives individuals to achieve greatness against all odds. It's the force that transforms dreams into reality, ideas into inventions, and challenges into triumphs. But why is persistence so powerful? The answer lies not only in motivational speeches but also in the solid ground of science.

Neuroscience shows us that every time we persist through a challenge, our brain adapts and strengthens. This process, known as neuroplasticity, means that with each effort, we become more capable of facing future challenges. Psychologically, persistence is linked to the growth mindset, a concept introduced by psychologist Carol Dweck. Individuals with a growth mindset believe that their abilities can improve over time with effort, leading to higher levels of achievement and resilience.

The Challenges of Developing Persistence
Developing persistence is akin to training for a marathon. It requires patience, practice, and a deep understanding of one's own motivations and fears. The road is often speckled with obstacles, doubts, and failures. It's easy to feel discouraged when progress seems slow or invisible. Yet, it is precisely in these moments that the seeds of persistence are sown and nurtured.

The science of habit formation offers insights into building persistence. Habits are the building blocks of persistence, formed through the repetition of actions in response to cues, leading to rewards. By setting small, achievable goals and consistently meeting them, we reinforce the neural pathways associated with persistence.

Cultivating Persistence

Set Clear Goals:
Know what you're working towards. Clear goals provide direction and a sense of purpose.

Embrace Failure:
View each setback as an opportunity to learn and grow. Failure is feedback, not a final verdict.

Celebrate Small Wins:
Acknowledge and celebrate your progress. This reinforces motivation and builds confidence.

Find Your Why:
Understanding why you're pursuing a goal can provide the fuel to keep going when the going gets tough.

Build a Support System:
Surround yourself with people who believe in you and your vision. A strong support system can provide encouragement and perspective.

Practice Self-Compassion:
Be kind to yourself. Persistence is a journey, not a sprint, and self-compassion is crucial for the long haul.

Stay Flexible:
Be willing to adjust your methods and strategies. Flexibility in approach ensures that you remain committed to your goal, even when faced with obstacles.

Break Tasks into Smaller Steps:
Large goals can be overwhelming. Break them down into smaller, manageable tasks. This makes it easier to start and maintain momentum, as each small step completed fuels your motivation to take on the next.

Maintain a Positive Attitude:
Your attitude plays a crucial role in persistence. Cultivate a positive mindset by focusing on solutions rather than problems. Positive thinking will help you navigate through tough times without losing hope or enthusiasm.

Use Visualization Techniques:
Visualize achieving your goals. This mental rehearsal can enhance your motivation and reinforce the belief in your ability to succeed, making persistence more natural.

Develop a Routine:
Consistency is key to building persistence. Establish a routine that includes dedicated time for working towards your goals. A consistent approach solidifies habits that contribute to persistence.

Limit Distractions:
Identify what commonly distracts you from your goals and find ways to minimize these interruptions. A focused environment helps maintain the discipline necessary for persistence.

Practice Gratitude:
Regularly reflect on what you're thankful for, including past successes and learning experiences. Gratitude can shift your perspective, making challenges seem more manageable and less daunting.

Seek Inspiration:
Look for stories of people who have achieved their goals through persistence. Learning about others' journeys can inspire you and provide practical insights into overcoming obstacles.

Strengthen Your Willpower:
Willpower is like a muscle; it becomes stronger with use. Practice self-control in various aspects of your life to enhance your ability to persist when faced with challenges.

Adopt a Learning Mindset:
View every experience as an opportunity to learn. This mindset encourages you to persist through difficulties because each challenge becomes a chance to grow.

Reward Yourself:
Set up a system to reward yourself for milestones reached. Rewards can reinforce your motivation and make the process of persisting more enjoyable.

Reflect and Adjust:
Regularly reflect on your progress and be willing to adjust your strategies. Flexibility in how you achieve your goals is crucial for sustaining persistence.

Build Physical Resilience:
Physical health impacts mental stamina. Regular exercise, adequate sleep, and healthy eating can enhance your physical resilience, making it easier to persist through mental and emotional challenges.

Learn to Manage Stress:
Develop stress management techniques such as deep breathing, meditation, or yoga. Managing stress effectively prevents burnout and helps maintain the mental clarity needed for persistence.

Connect with Your Passions:
Aligning your goals with your passions can naturally boost your motivation and persistence. When you're passionate about what you're pursuing, persisting becomes a labor of love rather than a chore.

Cultivate Patience:
Understand that success often takes time. Cultivating patience helps you to keep going even when progress seems slow, recognizing that persistence will eventually lead to achievement.

Conclusion

Developing persistence is a deeply personal and transformative journey. It's about discovering your strength, facing your fears, and emerging victorious, not despite the challenges but because of them. Remember, persistence is the thread that weaves through the fabric of all great achievements. It's the quiet determination that, day by day, turns the impossible into the inevitable. Embrace persistence, and watch as the doors of opportunity swing wide open, inviting you to step through to your fullest potential.

Developing a Sense of Humor

A sense of humor is the golden thread that adds vibrancy, resilience, and connection. It's the spark that can illuminate the darkest rooms, the balm that soothes the deepest wounds, and the bridge that connects disparate hearts. Cultivating a sense of humor is not merely about becoming the life of the party; it's about enriching your life's experience, enhancing your well-being, and navigating the world with a lighter heart and an open mind.

The Science of Laughter
Laughter, the most immediate manifestation of humor, is more than just a physical response to something funny. Scientifically, it's a potent tool for health, social bonding, and psychological well-being. Neurologically, laughter activates multiple regions of the brain, including those responsible for motor functions, emotion, and cognitive processing. This activation releases a cocktail of hormones and neurotransmitters, like endorphins, the body's natural painkillers, and dopamine, a key component in the reward and pleasure centers of the brain.

Psychologically, humor and laughter have been linked to increased resilience. They act as a buffer against stress, reducing the levels of stress hormones like cortisol and adrenaline in the body. Socially, laughter is contagious; it creates a shared experience that can break down barriers, foster connections, and build trust within groups. A sense of humor can therefore be seen as a social glue, bonding individuals through shared moments of joy and levity.

Cultivating Your Sense of Humor

Seek Out Humor:
Start by integrating more humor into your daily life. Watch comedies, listen to humorous podcasts, or read funny books. Surrounding yourself with humor can naturally influence your perspective.

Laugh at Yourself:
Learning to laugh at your own mistakes and quirks is a sign of self-acceptance and confidence. It demonstrates resilience and the ability to navigate life's imperfections with grace.

Connect with Funny People:
Spend time with those who bring joy and laughter into your life. Humor is contagious, and these interactions can inspire you to view life through a humorous lens.

Practice Humor:
Humor is a skill that can be honed. Try incorporating light-hearted comments into conversations, tell jokes, or share amusing observations. It's okay if not everything lands perfectly; humor is subjective, and the act of trying can itself be a source of amusement.

Learn the Art of Timing:
Much of humor is about timing. Observing comedic timing in movies, stand-up comedy, or even in conversations can help you understand when to introduce humor for the greatest effect.

Embrace Different Types of Humor:
Humor comes in many forms, from wit and wordplay to observational comedy. Explore various types to find what resonates most with you and your audience.

Use Humor to Cope:
Use humor as a tool to deal with life's challenges. A humorous perspective can make problems seem more manageable and less intimidating.

The Impact of a Humorous Outlook
Developing a sense of humor is akin to learning a new language—the language of joy, resilience, and humanity. It's about seeing the light in the shadows, finding joy in the journey, and spreading warmth in a

world that can sometimes feel cold and disconnected. A well-developed sense of humor is a source of strength, a means of connection, and a pathway to a richer, more fulfilling life.

Conclusion

Humor is much more than mere jokes; it's a perspective on life, a way of being in the world. It's about transforming the ordinary into the extraordinary, finding happiness in the mundane, and always keeping the light of laughter burning bright within your heart. As you navigate the ups and downs of life, let humor be your guide, your solace, and your way back to joy.

Dealing with Peer Pressure

In the journey of life, peer pressure is like a crosswind that tries to steer us off our chosen path. It's the push from those around us to act, think, or feel in ways that may not align with our values or desires. While it's a common experience across all ages, mastering the art of dealing with peer pressure is a testament to one's strength, courage, and commitment to personal integrity.

Understanding Peer Pressure
Peer pressure isn't just about being coerced into trying something harmful; it's about the subtler, often overlooked nudges towards conformity. Science helps us understand why we're so susceptible to it. Our brains are wired to belong, with social acceptance being a core human need. Studies in social psychology highlight that the fear of rejection activates the same areas of the brain associated with physical pain, suggesting why we often go to great lengths to fit in.

However, succumbing to peer pressure can lead to a loss of individuality, regret, and even resentment. It can derail us from our goals, compromise our values, and lead to behavior that conflicts with our sense of self.

The Power of No
Learning to say "no" is a powerful skill in combating peer pressure. It's not about defiance but about honoring your values and choices. Saying no requires understanding your worth and recognizing that your respect for yourself outweighs the desire for external approval. It's a declaration that you are the author of your life story.

Embracing Your Individuality
Your uniqueness is your superpower. Embracing your individuality means celebrating what makes you different and resisting the urge to blend into the crowd. It's about being proud of who you are and where

you're headed. When you're confident in your identity, peer pressure loses its grip, and you become a leader rather than a follower.

Strategies to Stand Firm
Know Your Values: Clear values act as a compass that guides your decisions. Knowing what you stand for makes it easier to resist peer pressure that contradicts your principles.

Build Self-Esteem:
High self-esteem acts as a shield against peer pressure. When you value yourself, you're less likely to seek validation from others.

Choose Your Company Wisely:
Surround yourself with people who respect your choices and encourage you to be your best self. Positive social circles reinforce your strength to resist negative peer pressure.

Practice Assertiveness:
Assertiveness is expressing your thoughts and feelings confidently and respectfully. It's about being firm in your decisions without being aggressive.

Visualize Success:
Use visualization to strengthen your resolve. Imagine yourself standing firm in your decisions and the positive outcomes of doing so.

Educate Yourself:
Knowledge is power. Understanding the consequences of giving into peer pressure can motivate you to stay true to your path.

Seek Support:
Don't hesitate to reach out to someone you trust when facing peer pressure. A supportive friend, family member, or mentor can offer advice and reinforcement.

Experiences That Forge a Man

Becoming a man of character and substance isn't an event but a journey shaped by a mosaic of experiences. These experiences, both challenging and uplifting, act as the anvil and hammer in the forge of personal growth, molding character, resilience, and wisdom. This chapter explores pivotal experiences that contribute significantly to the journey of manhood, offering insights into how these moments refine and define the essence of a man.

1. Overcoming Adversity
Facing and overcoming challenges is a cornerstone experience in the development of resilience and grit. Adversity, whether in the form of personal loss, failure, or hardship, teaches invaluable lessons about perseverance, strength, and the capacity for recovery. Scientific research underscores the concept of post-traumatic growth, illustrating how individuals often emerge from difficult periods with increased personal strength, a deeper appreciation for life, and a redefined sense of priorities.

2. Pursuing Passion and Purpose
Discovering and pursuing one's passion and purpose stands as a pivotal chapter in a man's life. This pursuit is not just about career success but finding meaning and fulfillment in activities that resonate with one's core values and aspirations. The journey toward realizing one's purpose is backed by psychological research indicating that individuals with a strong sense of purpose tend to have higher well-being, life satisfaction, and even longevity.

3. Building and Nurturing Relationships
The relationships a man builds and nurtures throughout his life—be they familial, platonic, or romantic—play a significant role in shaping his character. These relationships teach empathy, understanding, and the value of connection. They also offer opportunities for personal

reflection and growth, as each relationship acts as a mirror reflecting back aspects of oneself that may need attention or development.

4. Embracing Leadership and Responsibility

Taking on roles of leadership and responsibility, whether in one's personal life, community, or workplace, cultivates a sense of accountability and service. Leadership experiences challenge men to grow, make difficult decisions, and consider the welfare of others alongside their own. The act of serving and leading others fosters a deep sense of fulfillment and contributes to the development of integrity and ethical standards.

5. Experiencing Failure and Learning from It

Failure, though often feared, is a powerful teacher. It tests resilience, flexibility, and the willingness to persevere. Experiencing failure and learning to view it as a stepping stone rather than a setback is crucial for personal growth. Psychological studies highlight the importance of developing a growth mindset, wherein challenges and failures are seen as opportunities for learning and development.

6. Cultivating Self-awareness and Reflection

Periods of solitude and reflection are essential for cultivating self-awareness. They provide the space to introspect, understand one's thoughts, emotions, and behaviors, and align one's actions with personal values and goals. This self-awareness is foundational for emotional intelligence, a key predictor of success and satisfaction in various aspects of life.

7. Engaging with Cultures and Perspectives Beyond One's Own

Traveling or engaging with cultures and perspectives different from one's own broadens horizons, challenges preconceptions, and fosters a sense of global citizenship. These experiences cultivate empathy, adaptability, and an appreciation for the diverse tapestry of human experience.

Conclusion

The path to manhood is marked by a series of transformative experiences that challenge, teach, and inspire. Embracing these experiences with courage, openness, and a willingness to learn is key to forging a character of depth and integrity. Each man's journey is unique, yet the essence of what it means to become a man of substance remains rooted in the universal themes of growth, resilience, empathy, and purpose.

Remember, becoming a man isn't about reaching a destination; it's about the continual process of becoming better—better than you were yesterday, more understanding, more compassionate, and more aligned with your deepest values. It's a journey worth embarking on, with every step offering the opportunity to forge the legacy of who you choose to be.

Leaving a Legacy

Leaving a legacy is about creating ripples that extend far beyond the immediate shores of our own lives. It's about the mark we leave on the world, the imprint of our actions, decisions, and essence on the fabric of time. For a man, crafting a legacy is not about monumental achievements or worldly accolades; it's about living a life that resonates with purpose, integrity, and impact. It's about building a narrative of your existence that continues to inspire, motivate, and uplift long after your physical presence has faded.

Crafting a Life Worth Remembering
To create a life you can look back on with pride is to live deliberately and with conviction. Every man has the potential to build a legacy, but it requires conscious effort and unwavering commitment to the values and principles that define you. It's about making choices that align with your true self, not just following the crowd or trying to please everyone. Science tells us that authenticity leads to a more fulfilling and happier life. When you are true to yourself, you are more likely to engage in activities that bring you joy and fulfillment, paving the way for a legacy built on genuine happiness and achievement.

The Science of Legacy
Neuroscience research shows that our actions and decisions shape our brain's neural pathways, reinforcing behaviors and habits that define our character. The legacy you leave is essentially the sum of these behaviors and habits, as observed and remembered by those whose lives you've touched. Psychological studies also highlight the importance of social connections and community involvement in legacy building. Positive relationships and contributions to society are consistently linked with a more meaningful and lasting legacy.

Living a life true to your values and beliefs is also crucial for mental health. Studies in positive psychology affirm that individuals who live in alignment with their core values experience higher levels of well-being and life satisfaction. These findings underscore the significance of living authentically, not just for the sake of your legacy, but for your immediate happiness and health.

How to Leave a Legacy

Live Authentically:
Be true to yourself. Your legacy is a reflection of your true identity, not a mask worn to please others.

Prioritize Relationships:
The quality of your relationships is the true measure of your legacy. Nurture connections that enrich your life and the lives of others.

Make a Difference:
Seek out ways to contribute to your community and the world. Big or small, acts of service leave lasting imprints.

Embrace Learning and Growth:
View life as a continuous journey of learning. Share your knowledge and experiences to inspire and educate others.

Express Gratitude:
Appreciate the beauty in your life and the people in it. Gratitude amplifies the positive impact of your actions.

Document Your Journey:
Keep a journal, write letters, or record stories. These personal artifacts can be invaluable to those you leave behind.

Live with Purpose:
Identify what you're passionate about and pursue it with all your heart. A life lived with purpose is inherently impactful.

Conclusion

The legacy of a man is etched not in stone monuments but in the hearts and minds of those he's touched with his actions, words, and essence. It's a tapestry woven from moments of courage, acts of kindness, and a commitment to living a life of meaning and purpose. Remember, it's never too early or too late to start building your legacy. Every day is an opportunity to add another stroke to the masterpiece that is your life. Live in such a way that when you look back, you can say with certainty, "I lived, I loved, I mattered."

A Man's Happiness

Happiness, a seemingly elusive goal, remains at the heart of what many consider a life well-lived. For men, the pursuit of happiness can be shaped by various factors—personal achievements, relationships, fulfillment of duties, and the joy of discovery. This chapter delves into the multifaceted nature of happiness in men's lives, exploring the scientific underpinnings, societal expectations, and personal journeys that define and drive their quest for joy.

The Components of Happiness in Men

Happiness in men, as in all people, is a complex interplay of biological, psychological, and social factors. Understanding these components can illuminate pathways to a more fulfilled and contented life.

Biological Foundations:
Neuroscientific research highlights the role of neurotransmitters such as dopamine and serotonin in feeling pleasure and satisfaction. Physical activities, especially those that challenge the body, can elevate these chemicals, contributing to a sense of well-being.

Psychological Fulfillment:
Psychological theories, such as Maslow's hierarchy of needs, suggest that beyond basic physiological and safety needs, men (like all individuals) seek belonging, esteem, and ultimately self-actualization. Achieving goals, mastering skills, and realizing personal potential are pivotal in this pursuit.

Social Connections:
Strong social bonds are consistently linked to happiness. Relationships with family, friends, and romantic partners provide support, love, and a sense of belonging. For many men, the fulfillment derived from being a dependable partner, friend, and community member is a significant source of joy.

Achieving Happiness

Understanding what contributes to happiness lays the groundwork for strategies to enhance it. Here are actionable insights based on scientific research and psychological practice:

Pursue Meaningful Goals:
Engaging in work or hobbies that are meaningful and challenging can lead to a state known as "flow," where individuals lose themselves in the activity, leading to intrinsic happiness.

Cultivate Relationships:
Investing time and effort into building and maintaining relationships is crucial. Acts of kindness, active listening, and sharing experiences can deepen connections and foster happiness.

Practice Gratitude and Mindfulness:
Regularly acknowledging what you're thankful for and staying present can shift perspectives from what's lacking to appreciating what's available, enhancing feelings of contentment.

Embrace Emotional Expression:
Allowing oneself to express and experience a full range of emotions, including vulnerability, can lead to deeper interpersonal connections and personal growth.

Maintain Physical Health:
Exercise, a balanced diet, and sufficient sleep not only improve physical health but have been shown to have a positive impact on mental well-being.

Navigating Societal Expectations

Men often face societal pressures to conform to certain ideals of success and stoicism. Recognizing and navigating these expectations—choosing which to embrace and which to redefine on personal terms—is essential for authentic happiness.

Redefine Success:
Success is subjective. For some, it may be career advancement; for others, personal growth or community service. Defining success on your own terms is key to fulfillment.

Balance Strength with Vulnerability:
Strength is not just physical or emotional stoicism but includes the courage to be vulnerable and seek support when needed.

Conclusion

Happiness is not a one-size-fits-all formula but a personal journey that evolves. For men seeking happiness, it involves understanding oneself, pursuing passions, forging meaningful relationships, and contributing positively to the lives of others. It's about creating a life that reflects individual values, aspirations, and definitions of joy.

In this quest, science offers valuable insights, but personal experiences and emotions pave the path. Each man's journey to happiness is unique, filled with its own challenges, triumphs, and discoveries. Embracing this journey with openness, curiosity, and resilience can lead to a deeply satisfying and joyful life.

Do Something

In the journey toward manhood and personal fulfillment, hesitation is often the barrier that stands between dreams and reality. This chapter, titled "Do Something," is a clarion call to all men who aspire to achieve, to step into the arena of action today, not tomorrow. It's about breaking free from the shackles of procrastination and the paralysis of indecision. It's about recognizing that the power to change, to grow, and to conquer lies in the immediate, tangible actions you take right now.

The Psychology of Action

Why do we wait? Why do we let precious moments slip by, waiting for the "perfect" time that never comes? Psychological research into procrastination sheds light on this, identifying fear of failure, fear of success, and a lack of self-discipline as key culprits. Yet, the science of behavioral psychology also offers us a way out: the principle of "just do it." Studies show that taking even the smallest step towards a goal can catalyze a chain reaction of further action, thanks to the momentum it generates and the positive reinforcement it brings.

Overcoming Fear:
Fear, whether of failure or judgment, is a significant barrier to action. Combat this by breaking your goal into smaller, manageable tasks. The act of achieving these smaller goals can boost your confidence, reduce fear, and foster a sense of momentum.

The Power of Now:
Neuroscience tells us that making a decision and taking action activates the brain's reward pathways, releasing dopamine—a neurotransmitter associated with feelings of pleasure and satisfaction. This biological response can be harnessed to fuel further action and decision-making.

Embrace the Journey of Doing

Start Today:
The perfect time is a myth. The best time to start is now. Whether it's signing up for kickboxing lessons because you want to feel more confident in your ability to defend yourself or beginning that project you've always dreamed of, the act of starting immediately breaks the inertia of procrastination.

Make the Call:
If you're contemplating taking a new class, learning a new skill, or reaching out for opportunities, make the call now. Action breeds confidence, not the other way around. Every step you take builds a bridge to your goals.

Accept Imperfection:
Waiting for the perfect moment or the perfect plan often means waiting forever. Accept that initial efforts may be imperfect but see this as a part of the learning process. Progress, not perfection, is the goal.

Find Accountability:
Share your goals with someone you trust, or even better, find someone who shares your aspirations. Accountability can significantly increase your chances of taking action and sticking with it.

The Ripple Effect of Action

Taking action, no matter how small, sets off a ripple effect that can transform your life. It's not just about the immediate results but about the person you become in the process: more confident, resilient, and empowered. Action propels you from a state of dreaming to a state of doing, from aspiring to achieving.

Builds Self-Respect:
Every action you take in the direction of your goals builds self-respect and self-esteem. It's a testament to your commitment to yourself and your future.

Creates Momentum:
Each action creates momentum, making subsequent actions easier and more effective. Like a snowball rolling down a hill, the size and speed of your progress will grow exponentially.

Conclusion: The Call to Action

The journey to achieving your dreams and becoming the man you aspire to be is paved with action. Remember, the difference between who you are and who you want to be lies in what you do. Don't let fear or procrastination hold you back. Embrace the power of now, take that first step, and never look back. Do something today that your future self will thank you for. Your journey of action starts now. Make it count.

Inspiring Movies

In the grand tapestry of storytelling, classic movies hold a special place, offering not just entertainment but profound lessons that resonate through generations. This chapter embarks on a journey through the world of classic cinema, exploring the timeless messages these films convey and how they continue to inspire and shape the character of men today. Through motivational insights and reflections, we delve into the core themes of these cinematic masterpieces and uncover the wisdom they offer for personal growth, resilience, and understanding the complexities of life.

The Power of Storytelling Through Cinema

Cinema, one of the most influential art forms of the 20th and 21st centuries, combines visual storytelling with compelling narratives that reflect the human condition. Classic movies, in particular, have the unique ability to capture the essence of their times while addressing universal themes such as courage, love, sacrifice, and redemption. These films serve as cultural touchstones, offering insights into the challenges and aspirations that define the human experience.

Classic Movies and Their Enduring Messages

"To Kill a Mockingbird" (1962) - The Importance of Integrity and Empathy: This film, based on Harper Lee's novel, teaches the importance of standing up for what is right, even when faced with widespread opposition. It underscores the value of empathy, understanding, and the fight against injustice, encouraging men to be champions of equity and compassion in their lives.

"It's a Wonderful Life" (1946) - The Impact of One Life on Many: A timeless tale of despair, redemption, and the realization of one's worth, this movie highlights how interconnected our lives are and the profound impact one individual can have on the community. It motivates men to recognize their value and the difference they can make.

"The Godfather" (1972) - The Complexity of Loyalty and Power: Beyond its portrayal of crime and ambition, this epic saga delves into themes of loyalty, family, and the burdens of leadership. It explores the complex balance between personal ethics and the demands of loyalty, offering a nuanced view of power and its effects on relationships and integrity.

"Casablanca" (1942) - The Sacrifice for Love and Greater Good: Set against the backdrop of World War II, this film navigates the themes of love, sacrifice, and the choices that define us. It teaches that sometimes, the greatest act of love is letting go for the greater good, a poignant message about the nature of selfless love and heroism.

"12 Angry Men" (1957) - The Significance of Justice and Dialogue: A compelling study of consensus-building and the pursuit of justice within a jury room, this film underscores the importance of dialogue, critical thinking, and the courage to stand alone against the crowd for the truth. It exemplifies the power of reasoned discussion and the impact of a single, principled voice.

Learning from Classic Cinema

Engaging with classic movies allows men to reflect on their own lives, values, and the legacies they wish to create. These films offer more than just historical snapshots; they provide timeless lessons on courage, love, responsibility, and the complexity of human emotions and ethics.

Cultivating Growth Through Cinema

Reflect on the Messages:
After watching a classic film, take time to reflect on its themes and messages. How do they apply to your life? What lessons can you draw from the characters' journeys?

Discuss with Others:
Conversations about films can deepen understanding and offer new perspectives. Share your thoughts with friends or family and explore different interpretations and insights.

Incorporate Lessons into Daily Life:
Consider how the virtues and challenges depicted in these movies relate to your personal growth, relationships, and professional life. Use these reflections as a source of inspiration and guidance.

Conclusion

Classic movies remain a rich source of wisdom, entertainment, and inspiration. For the modern man, they offer valuable lessons on character, resilience, and the human spirit. By engaging with these timeless tales, you can gain insights into navigating the complexities of life with grace, strength, and a deeper understanding of the world and your place within it.

Remember, the stories of yesterday have much to teach us about today and tomorrow. Let the classic cinema be a guide, a muse, and a reflection of the best within and all around us.

When to Start Dating?

Beginning the journey of dating and seeking a romantic partner is a significant step in a man's life. It's not just about finding someone who complements and enriches your life but also about being in the right place personally to begin this journey together. This chapter explores the foundational aspects that men should consider to be ready for dating, emphasizing the importance of personal development, financial stability, and emotional readiness. It's about ensuring you are ready to not just meet someone but to build a meaningful and lasting connection.

Building the Foundation: Self-Preparation Before Dating

Personal Development:
Before stepping into the dating world, it's crucial to have a strong sense of self. This involves understanding your values, goals, and what you're looking for in a partner. It also means cultivating a fulfilling life as a single person, including hobbies, interests, and friendships that bring you joy and fulfillment.

Financial Stability:
While love is not about financial transactions, financial stability is important in the context of dating and future partnerships. Being financially stable means having the means to participate in dating activities, yes, but it also signals the ability to contribute to a future shared life. This doesn't mean you need to be wealthy, but rather responsible and in control of your finances, with a stable foundation from which to build a future.

Emotional Maturity:
Emotional readiness is key to a healthy relationship. This means being able to manage your emotions, communicate effectively, and handle the ups and downs of dating with maturity. It's about being ready to

invest emotionally in someone else and being open to the vulnerabilities that come with close relationships.

Life Experience:
Life experiences enrich your perspective and make you a more interesting and empathetic partner. Whether it's travel, learning, overcoming challenges, or personal achievements, these experiences contribute to your growth and readiness for a relationship.

Checklist: Am I Ready to Start Dating?

- ☐ Do I have qualities that are attractive to a woman?
- ☐ Can I take care of myself and someone else?
- ☐ Am I financially stable?
- ☐ Do I have something going for myself?
- ☐ Do I have enough life experience to be interesting?
- ☐ Do I know what to look for in a woman?
- ☐ Can I protect a woman?
- ☐ Am I effectively managing my personal problems?
- ☐ Do I know what my value is?

The Path to Readiness

Dating and relationships are significant aspects of life's journey, offering opportunities for joy, growth, and companionship. Preparing yourself for this journey is about more than ticking boxes; it's about building a life that you're proud of and ready to share with someone else. By focusing on personal development, financial stability, emotional maturity, and gaining life experience, you set the foundation for a healthy, fulfilling relationship.

Remember, the right time to start dating is when you feel prepared not just to find love but to give it, to share your life, and to begin the adventure of partnership with openness, responsibility, and commitment.

What to look for in a woman?

In the journey of life, finding a partner who complements and enriches your existence is a quest that many embark on. This chapter explores key qualities that form the foundation of a deep, lasting relationship, going beyond surface attributes to underscore the essence of what makes a connection truly rewarding.

Innocence
Seek a partner that didn't sleep with a lot of men. High Body counts are an indication of a lack of impulse control, no self-respect, instability in a relationship or emotional and psychological problems, all of which are dealbreakers in relationships. A woman with a high body count isn't going to be a faithful, long-term partner. Also, make sure she's not posting any provocative images on her social media or any other kind of attention seeking pictures or videos.

Caring Nature:
A caring partner, who shows genuine concern and kindness, not only enriches your life but also has the potential to be a nurturing presence in the lives of any future family. This quality is foundational for building a supportive and loving home environment.

Supportive of Goals:
Look for someone who understands and supports your ambitions and dreams. A supportive partner encourages you in facing challenges and celebrates your successes, offering motivation and understanding on your path to achieving personal and shared goals.

Valuing Intellectual and Emotional Depth

Intelligence:
Intelligence, both emotional and intellectual, is vital. A partner who is curious, thoughtful, and keen to engage in meaningful conversations

brings a stimulating dynamic to the relationship, fostering a connection that goes beyond the superficial.

Honesty and Integrity:
Honesty builds trust, the cornerstone of any strong relationship. A partner who values integrity and communicates truthfully fosters a safe and open environment for both partners to express themselves authentically.

Respect:
Mutual respect is non-negotiable, but a good woman is respectful towards men (men deserving of respect).

Empathy:
The ability to understand and share the feelings of another is at the heart of empathy. A partner who empathizes can connect on a deep emotional level, offering support and understanding through life's ups and downs.

Checklist: Is she wifey material?

- ☐ She has a low body count or none at all.
- ☐ She has no provocative images on her social media.
- ☐ She respects men (men deserving of respect)
- ☐ She has a lot of feminine traits.
- ☐ She has self-respect.
- ☐ She makes sure she looks good.
- ☐ She is caring and could be a great mother.
- ☐ She is supportive.
- ☐ She lets you be a man.
- ☐ She doesn't have a lot of male friends.

How to Behave Around a Woman?

In the journey of forming meaningful connections with women, it's essential to strike a balance between respect, independence, and authenticity. The essence of your interactions should pivot around mutual respect and understanding, rather than adhering to outdated stereotypes or social media trends. Here, we delve into a guide crafted to navigate these interactions thoughtfully, blending emotional intelligence with behavioral science.

Don't Be Needy:
The principle of not being needy stems from a broader understanding of human psychology. Science indicates that individuals who exhibit self-sufficiency and confidence tend to be more attractive. This is rooted in evolutionary psychology, where traits such as independence and self-reliance are seen as indicators of a strong mate. It's not about distancing yourself emotionally but showcasing that your happiness and well-being are not solely dependent on others.

Be a Gentleman:
The act of paying for dinners, opening doors, or generally being courteous is often associated with the traditional notion of being a gentleman. But let's delve deeper into why these gestures matter. Psychological studies suggest that altruism (the selfless concern for the well-being of others) plays a crucial role in human relationships. It signals to the other person that you are capable of caring and providing support. These actions, when genuine, foster a sense of safety and respect. However, it's crucial to recognize that these gestures should be motivated by genuine care rather than obligation or expectation of reciprocity.

Taking the Lead:
Taking the lead in decisions is often misconstrued as being controlling, yet there's a fine line between assertiveness and dominance. The idea here is to show confidence in making decisions, which can be reassuring to your partner. It ties back to the concept of perceived competence and leadership in evolutionary psychology, where decision-making ability is linked to resourcefulness and security. However, this doesn't negate the importance of mutual agreement and respecting your partner's opinions and desires.

Moderation in Compliments:
While it may seem counterintuitive, the science behind giving fewer compliments is rooted in the psychological principle of scarcity. When compliments are rare, they become more meaningful and are perceived as more sincere. Over-complimenting can sometimes lead to the devaluation of your words, making them seem insincere or performative. Authenticity in your admiration makes your compliments more impactful and cherished.

Avoiding the "Simp" Behavior:
The term "simp" has gained traction on social media, often used to describe someone who goes overboard in their admiration or submission to someone else, typically without reciprocation. From a psychological standpoint, this behavior can stem from a lack of self-esteem and an excessive need for approval. Healthy relationships are built on mutual respect and equality, where both individuals value and appreciate each other without one having to undermine their self-worth.

Emotional Resonance:
Incorporating these behaviors into your interactions with women should be driven by a genuine desire to connect and form meaningful relationships, not merely to adhere to societal expectations or to manipulate emotions. It's about respecting their autonomy, valuing their presence in your life, and fostering a partnership based on equality and mutual support. This approach not only enriches your relationships but also contributes to your personal growth and emotional well-being.

Conclusion

As we navigate the complexities of human relationships, it's essential to remember that the foundation of any meaningful connection is respect, empathy, and genuine affection. By understanding the psychological principles behind our behaviors and interactions, we can strive to create relationships that are not only fulfilling but also respectful and enriching. Let this chapter serve as a guide to cultivating relationships with women that are based on mutual respect, understanding, and genuine care. Embrace the journey of learning, growth, and emotional connection as you move forward in your interactions.

Checklist: Am I a good man?

- ☐ I have high testosterone.
- ☐ I am not fat.
- ☐ I'm working out or something similar.
- ☐ I have muscle.
- ☐ I have like-minded friends around me.
- ☐ I'm using social media for business purposes.
- ☐ I don't post 'simp' comments.
- ☐ I don't follow female models or female celebrities.
- ☐ I'm not showing off on social media.
- ☐ I'm not looking for validation on social media.
- ☐ I'm a busy person.
- ☐ I have a hobby or passion.
- ☐ I'm conquering my fears.
- ☐ I'm confident and it's not based on external things.
- ☐ I'm masculine.
- ☐ I'm loyal
- ☐ I'm stoic
- ☐ I have a purpose in my life.
- ☐ I take care of myself.
- ☐ I can be alone if I wanted to.
- ☐ I've been through some hardships in my life.
- ☐ I took and can take risks.
- ☐ I'm not a pleaser (I can say no)
- ☐ I'm financially stable.
- ☐ I'm trying to become smarter each day.
- ☐ I have life experience.
- ☐ I'm not watching porn.
- ☐ I can adapt to new situations.

- ☐ I can be patient.
- ☐ I can make quick rational decisions.
- ☐ I can be a leader (I have the skills for it)
- ☐ I'm good at storytelling (Communicating)
- ☐ I'm and can be independent.
- ☐ I can negotiate.
- ☐ I'm a critical thinker.
- ☐ I have full emotional control.
- ☐ I have a positive mindset.
- ☐ I'm persistent.
- ☐ I'm disciplined.
- ☐ I have a sense of humor.
- ☐ I can deal with peer pressure.
- ☐ I'm responsible.
- ☐ I'm trying to leave a legacy.
- ☐ I don't wait to get something done.
- ☐ I know what to look for in a woman.
- ☐ I'm not needy or simping.
- ☐ I know my own value.
- ☐ I have qualities that can attract a woman.
- ☐ I can protect a woman.
- ☐ I can the lead in a relationship.
- ☐ I don't eat any unhealthy food.
- ☐ I don't have addictions.
- ☐ I can handle stress.
- ☐ I'm emotional intelligent.

Join Our Mission to Empower Men!

Dear Valued Reader,

We trust that you found value and inspiration within the pages of this guide on embracing true masculinity. Crafting this book was a journey fueled by our passion to support men like you on the path to discovering and living out the fullness of your potential.

This book is a proud creation of **Skriuwer**, a global collective committed to producing content that transforms lives. Our mission is to offer insights that are not just thought-provoking but also actionable, guiding you towards becoming the man you aspire to be.

Your journey with us doesn't have to stop here. You are a vital member of our expanding community. If there's any aspect of the book that didn't resonate with you, or if you have ideas on how we can improve, we're here to listen. Reach out to us at **kontakt@skriuwer.com**. Your input is invaluable in our quest to continually enhance our offerings.

Did this book inspire you? Make your voice heard! We invite you to share your thoughts by leaving a review on the platform where you acquired this book. Your positive feedback not only motivates us but also aids others in discovering the resources they need to grow and thrive.

Thank you for choosing **Skriuwer**. Together, let's forge ahead on this remarkable journey of learning and self-discovery.

With Appreciation,
The Skriuwer Team

www.ingramcontent.com/pod-product-compliance
Lightning Source LLC
LaVergne TN
LVHW021052100526
838202LV00083B/5666